CSB
SCRIPTURE
NOTEBOOK

1 and 2 Samuel

Read. Reflect. Respond.

1 SAMUEL

Private

PS yes I am
talking to you ely
and carter.

Hannah's Vow

1 There was a man from Ramathaim-zophim in the hill country of Ephraim. His name was Elkanah son of Jeroham, son of Elihu, son of Tohu, son of Zuph, an Ephraimite. ² He had two wives, the first named Hannah and the second Peninnah. Peninnah had children, but Hannah was childless. ³ This man would go up from his town every year to worship and to sacrifice to the LORD of Armies at Shiloh, where Eli's two sons, Hophni and Phinehas, were the LORD's priests.

⁴ Whenever Elkanah offered a sacrifice, he always gave portions of the meat to his wife Peninnah and to each of her sons and daughters. ⁵ But he gave a double portion to Hannah, for he loved her even though the LORD had kept her from conceiving. ⁶ Her rival would taunt her severely just to provoke her, because the LORD had kept Hannah from conceiving. ⁷ Year after year, when she went up to the LORD's house, her rival taunted her in this way. Hannah would weep and would not eat. ⁸ "Hannah, why are you crying?" her husband, Elkanah, would ask. "Why won't you eat? Why are you troubled? Am I not better to you than ten sons?"

⁹ On one occasion, Hannah got up after they ate and drank at Shiloh. The priest Eli was sitting on a chair by the doorpost of the LORD's temple. ¹⁰ Deeply hurt, Hannah prayed to the LORD and wept with many tears. ¹¹ Making a vow, she pleaded, "LORD of Armies, if you will take notice of your servant's affliction, remember and not forget me, and give your servant a son, I will give him to the LORD all the days of his life, and his hair will never be cut."

¹² While she continued praying in the LORD's presence, Eli watched her mouth. ¹³ Hannah was praying silently, and though her lips were moving, her voice could not be heard. Eli thought she was drunk ¹⁴ and said to her, "How long are you going to be drunk? Get rid of your wine!"

Hannahs vow

there was a man from Rama thaim-Zophim in the Hill Country

¹⁵ "No, my lord," Hannah replied. "I am a woman with a broken heart. I haven't had any wine or beer; I've been pouring out my heart before the LORD. ¹⁶ Don't think of me as a wicked woman; I've been praying from the depth of my anguish and resentment."

¹⁷ Eli responded, "Go in peace, and may the God of Israel grant the request you've made of him."

¹⁸ "May your servant find favor with you," she replied. Then Hannah went on her way; she ate and no longer looked despondent.

Samuel's Birth and Dedication

¹⁹ The next morning Elkanah and Hannah got up early to worship before the LORD. Afterward, they returned home to Ramah. Then Elkanah was intimate with his wife Hannah, and the LORD remembered her. ²⁰ After some time, Hannah conceived and gave birth to a son. She named him Samuel, because she said, "I requested him from the LORD."

²¹ When Elkanah and all his household went up to make the annual sacrifice and his vow offering to the LORD, ²² Hannah did not go and explained to her husband, "After the child is weaned, I'll take him to appear in the LORD's presence and to stay there permanently."

²³ Her husband, Elkanah, replied, "Do what you think is best, and stay here until you've weaned him. May the LORD confirm your word." So Hannah stayed there and nursed her son until she weaned him. ²⁴ When she had weaned him, she took him with her to Shiloh, as well as a three-year-old bull, half a bushel of flour, and a clay jar of wine. Though the boy was still young, she took him to the LORD's house at Shiloh. ²⁵ Then they slaughtered the bull and brought the boy to Eli.

²⁶ "Please, my lord," she said, "as surely as you live, my lord, I am the woman who stood here beside you praying to the LORD.

²⁷ I prayed for this boy, and since the LORD gave me what I asked him for, ²⁸ I now give the boy to the LORD. For as long as he lives, he is given to the LORD." Then he worshiped the LORD there.

Hannah's Triumphant Prayer

2 Hannah prayed:
My heart rejoices in the LORD;
   my horn is lifted up by the LORD.
   My mouth boasts over my enemies,
   because I rejoice in your salvation.
² There is no one holy like the LORD.
   There is no one besides you!
   And there is no rock like our God.
³ Do not boast so proudly,
   or let arrogant words come out of your mouth,
   for the LORD is a God of knowledge,
   and actions are weighed by him.
⁴ The bows of the warriors are broken,
   but the feeble are clothed with strength.
⁵ Those who are full hire themselves out for food,
   but those who are starving hunger no more.
   The woman who is childless gives birth to seven,
   but the woman with many sons pines away.
⁶ The LORD brings death and gives life;
   he sends some down to Sheol, and he raises others up.
⁷ The LORD brings poverty and gives wealth;
   he humbles and he exalts.
⁸ He raises the poor from the dust
   and lifts the needy from the trash heap.
   He seats them with noblemen
   and gives them a throne of honor.
   For the foundations of the earth are the LORD's;
   he has set the world on them.

⁹ He guards the steps of his faithful ones,
but the wicked perish in darkness,
for a person does not prevail by his own strength.
¹⁰ Those who oppose the LORD will be shattered;
he will thunder in the heavens against them.
The LORD will judge the ends of the earth.
He will give power to his king;
he will lift up the horn of his anointed.

¹¹ Elkanah went home to Ramah, but the boy served the LORD in the presence of the priest Eli.

Eli's Family Judged

¹² Eli's sons were wicked men; they did not respect the LORD ¹³ or the priests' share of the sacrifices from the people. When anyone offered a sacrifice, the priest's servant would come with a three-pronged meat fork while the meat was boiling ¹⁴ and plunge it into the container, kettle, cauldron, or cooking pot. The priest would claim for himself whatever the meat fork brought up. This is the way they treated all the Israelites who came there to Shiloh. ¹⁵ Even before the fat was burned, the priest's servant would come and say to the one who was sacrificing, "Give the priest some meat to roast, because he won't accept boiled meat from you — only raw." ¹⁶ If that person said to him, "The fat must be burned first; then you can take whatever you want for yourself," the servant would reply, "No, I insist that you hand it over right now. If you don't, I'll take it by force!" ¹⁷ So the servants' sin was very severe in the presence of the LORD, because the men treated the LORD's offering with contempt.

¹⁸ Samuel served in the LORD's presence—this mere boy was dressed in the linen ephod. ¹⁹ Each year his mother made him a little robe and took it to him when she went with her husband

to offer the annual sacrifice. [20] Eli would bless Elkanah and his wife: "May the LORD give you children by this woman in place of the one she has given to the LORD." Then they would go home.

[21] The LORD paid attention to Hannah's need, and she conceived and gave birth to three sons and two daughters. Meanwhile, the boy Samuel grew up in the presence of the LORD.

[22] Now Eli was very old. He heard about everything his sons were doing to all Israel and how they were sleeping with the women who served at the entrance to the tent of meeting. [23] He said to them, "Why are you doing these things? I have heard about your evil actions from all these people. [24] No, my sons, the news I hear the LORD's people spreading is not good. [25] If one person sins against another, God can intercede for him, but if a person sins against the LORD, who can intercede for him?" But they would not listen to their father, since the LORD intended to kill them. [26] By contrast, the boy Samuel grew in stature and in favor with the LORD and with people.

[27] A man of God came to Eli and said to him, "This is what the LORD says: 'Didn't I reveal myself to your forefather's family when they were in Egypt and belonged to Pharaoh's palace? [28] Out of all the tribes of Israel, I chose your house to be my priests, to offer sacrifices on my altar, to burn incense, and to wear an ephod in my presence. I also gave your forefather's family all the Israelite food offerings. [29] Why, then, do all of you despise my sacrifices and offerings that I require at the place of worship? You have honored your sons more than me, by making yourselves fat with the best part of all of the offerings of my people Israel.'

[30] "Therefore, this is the declaration of the LORD, the God of Israel: 'I did say that your family and your forefather's family would walk before me forever. But now,' this is the LORD's declaration, 'no longer! For those who honor me I will honor, but those who despise me will be disgraced. [31] Look, the days are

coming when I will cut off your strength and the strength of your forefather's family, so that none in your family will reach old age. ³² You will see distress in the place of worship, in spite of all that is good in Israel, and no one in your family will ever again reach old age. ³³ Any man from your family I do not cut off from my altar will bring grief and sadness to you. All your descendants will die violently. ³⁴ This will be the sign that will come to you concerning your two sons Hophni and Phinehas: both of them will die on the same day.

³⁵ " 'Then I will raise up a faithful priest for myself. He will do whatever is in my heart and mind. I will establish a lasting dynasty for him, and he will walk before my anointed one for all time. ³⁶ Anyone who is left in your family will come and bow down to him for a piece of silver or a loaf of bread. He will say: Please appoint me to some priestly office so I can have a piece of bread to eat.' "

Samuel's Call

3 The boy Samuel served the LORD in Eli's presence. In those days the word of the LORD was rare and prophetic visions were not widespread.

² One day Eli, whose eyesight was failing, was lying in his usual place. ³ Before the lamp of God had gone out, Samuel was lying down in the temple of the LORD, where the ark of God was located.

⁴ Then the LORD called Samuel, and he answered, "Here I am." ⁵ He ran to Eli and said, "Here I am; you called me."

"I didn't call," Eli replied. "Go back and lie down." So he went and lay down.

⁶ Once again the LORD called, "Samuel! "

Samuel got up, went to Eli, and said, "Here I am; you called me."

"I didn't call, my son," he replied. "Go back and lie down."

⁷ Now Samuel did not yet know the LORD, because the word of the LORD had not yet been revealed to him. ⁸ Once again, for the third time, the LORD called Samuel. He got up, went to Eli, and said, "Here I am; you called me."

Then Eli understood that the LORD was calling the boy. ⁹ He told Samuel, "Go and lie down. If he calls you, say, 'Speak, LORD, for your servant is listening.'" So Samuel went and lay down in his place.

¹⁰ The LORD came, stood there, and called as before, "Samuel, Samuel!"

Samuel responded, "Speak, for your servant is listening."

¹¹ The LORD said to Samuel, "I am about to do something in Israel that will cause everyone who hears about it to shudder. ¹² On that day I will carry out against Eli everything I said about his family, from beginning to end. ¹³ I told him that I am going to judge his family forever because of the iniquity he knows about: his sons are cursing God, and he has not stopped them. ¹⁴ Therefore, I have sworn to Eli's family: The iniquity of Eli's family will never be wiped out by either sacrifice or offering."

¹⁵ Samuel lay down until the morning; then he opened the doors of the LORD's house. He was afraid to tell Eli the vision, ¹⁶ but Eli called him and said, "Samuel, my son."

"Here I am," answered Samuel.

¹⁷ "What was the message he gave you?" Eli asked. "Don't hide it from me. May God punish you and do so severely if you hide anything from me that he told you." ¹⁸ So Samuel told him everything and did not hide anything from him. Eli responded, "He is the LORD. Let him do what he thinks is good."

¹⁹ Samuel grew. The LORD was with him, and he fulfilled everything Samuel prophesied. ²⁰ All Israel from Dan to Beersheba knew that Samuel was a confirmed prophet of the LORD. ²¹ The LORD continued to appear in Shiloh, because there he

4 revealed himself to Samuel by his word. ¹And Samuel's words came to all Israel.

The Ark Captured by the Philistines

Israel went out to meet the Philistines in battle and camped at Ebenezer while the Philistines camped at Aphek. ²The Philistines lined up in battle formation against Israel, and as the battle intensified, Israel was defeated by the Philistines, who struck down about four thousand men on the battlefield.

³ When the troops returned to the camp, the elders of Israel asked, "Why did the LORD defeat us today before the Philistines? Let's bring the ark of the LORD's covenant from Shiloh. Then it will go with us and save us from our enemies." ⁴ So the people sent men to Shiloh to bring back the ark of the covenant of the LORD of Armies, who is enthroned between the cherubim. Eli's two sons, Hophni and Phinehas, were there with the ark of the covenant of God. ⁵ When the ark of the covenant of the LORD entered the camp, all the Israelites raised such a loud shout that the ground shook.

⁶ The Philistines heard the sound of the war cry and asked, "What's this loud shout in the Hebrews' camp?" When the Philistines discovered that the ark of the LORD had entered the camp, ⁷ they panicked. "A god has entered their camp!" they said. "Woe to us! Nothing like this has happened before. ⁸ Woe to us! Who will rescue us from these magnificent gods? These are the gods that slaughtered the Egyptians with all kinds of plagues in the wilderness. ⁹ Show some courage and be men, Philistines! Otherwise, you'll serve the Hebrews just as they served you. Now be men and fight!"

¹⁰ So the Philistines fought, and Israel was defeated, and each man fled to his tent. The slaughter was severe — thirty thousand of the Israelite foot soldiers fell. ¹¹ The ark of God was captured, and Eli's two sons, Hophni and Phinehas, died.

Eli's Death and Ichabod's Birth

¹² That same day, a Benjaminite man ran from the battle and came to Shiloh. His clothes were torn, and there was dirt on his head. ¹³ When he arrived, there was Eli sitting on his chair beside the road waiting, because he was anxious about the ark of God. When the man entered the city to give a report, the entire city cried out.

¹⁴ Eli heard the outcry and asked, "Why this commotion?" The man quickly came and reported to Eli. ¹⁵ At that time Eli was ninety-eight years old, and his eyes didn't move because he couldn't see.

¹⁶ The man said to Eli, "I'm the one who came from the battle. I fled from there today."

"What happened, my son?" Eli asked.

¹⁷ The messenger answered, "Israel has fled from the Philistines, and also there was a great slaughter among the people. Your two sons, Hophni and Phinehas, are both dead, and the ark of God has been captured." ¹⁸ When he mentioned the ark of God, Eli fell backward off the chair by the city gate, and since he was old and heavy, his neck broke and he died. Eli had judged Israel forty years.

¹⁹ Eli's daughter-in-law, the wife of Phinehas, was pregnant and about to give birth. When she heard the news about the capture of God's ark and the deaths of her father-in-law and her husband, she collapsed and gave birth because her labor pains came on her. ²⁰ As she was dying, the women taking care of her said, "Don't be afraid. You've given birth to a son!" But she did not respond or pay attention. ²¹ She named the boy Ichabod, saying, "The glory has departed from Israel," referring to the capture of the ark of God and to the deaths of her father-in-law and her husband. ²² "The glory has departed from Israel," she said, "because the ark of God has been captured."

The Ark in Philistine Hands

5 After the Philistines had captured the ark of God, they took it from Ebenezer to Ashdod, ² brought it into the temple of Dagon and placed it next to his statue. ³ When the people of Ashdod got up early the next morning, there was Dagon, fallen with his face to the ground before the ark of the LORD. So they took Dagon and returned him to his place. ⁴ But when they got up early the next morning, there was Dagon, fallen with his face to the ground before the ark of the LORD. This time, Dagon's head and both of his hands were broken off and lying on the threshold. Only Dagon's torso remained. ⁵ That is why, still today, the priests of Dagon and everyone who enters the temple of Dagon in Ashdod do not step on Dagon's threshold.

⁶ The LORD's hand was heavy on the people of Ashdod. He terrified the people of Ashdod and its territory and afflicted them with tumors. ⁷ When the people of Ashdod saw what was happening, they said, "The ark of Israel's God must not stay here with us, because his hand is strongly against us and our god Dagon." ⁸ So they called all the Philistine rulers together and asked, "What should we do with the ark of Israel's God?"

"The ark of Israel's God should be moved to Gath," they replied. So they moved the ark of Israel's God. ⁹ After they had moved it, the LORD's hand was against the city of Gath, causing a great panic. He afflicted the people of the city, from the youngest to the oldest, with an outbreak of tumors.

¹⁰ The people of Gath then sent the ark of God to Ekron, but when it got there, the Ekronites cried out, "They've moved the ark of Israel's God to us to kill us and our people!"

¹¹ The Ekronites called all the Philistine rulers together. They said, "Send the ark of Israel's God away. Let it return to its place so it won't kill us and our people!" For the fear of death pervaded the city; God's hand was oppressing them. ¹² Those who did

not die were afflicted with tumors, and the outcry of the city went up to heaven.

The Return of the Ark

6 When the ark of the LORD had been in Philistine territory for seven months, ² the Philistines summoned the priests and the diviners and pleaded, "What should we do with the ark of the LORD? Tell us how we can send it back to its place."

³ They replied, "If you send the ark of Israel's God away, do not send it without an offering. Send back a guilt offering to him, and you will be healed. Then the reason his hand hasn't been removed from you will be revealed."

⁴ They asked, "What guilt offering should we send back to him?"

And they answered, "Five gold tumors and five gold mice corresponding to the number of Philistine rulers, since there was one plague for both you and your rulers. ⁵ Make images of your tumors and of your mice that are destroying the land. Give glory to Israel's God, and perhaps he will stop oppressing you, your gods, and your land. ⁶ Why harden your hearts as the Egyptians and Pharaoh hardened theirs? When he afflicted them, didn't they send Israel away, and Israel left?

⁷ "Now then, prepare one new cart and two milk cows that have never been yoked. Hitch the cows to the cart, but take their calves away and pen them up. ⁸ Take the ark of the LORD, place it on the cart, and put the gold objects that you're sending him as a guilt offering in a box beside the ark. Send it off and let it go its way. ⁹ Then watch: If it goes up the road to its homeland toward Beth-shemesh, it is the LORD who has made this terrible trouble for us. However, if it doesn't, we will know that it was not his hand that punished us — it was just something that happened to us by chance."

¹⁰ The men did this: They took two milk cows, hitched them to the cart, and confined their calves in the pen. ¹¹ Then they put

the ark of the LORD on the cart, along with the box containing the gold mice and the images of their tumors. ¹² The cows went straight up the road to Beth-shemesh. They stayed on that one highway, lowing as they went; they never strayed to the right or to the left. The Philistine rulers were walking behind them to the territory of Beth-shemesh.

¹³ The people of Beth-shemesh were harvesting wheat in the valley, and when they looked up and saw the ark, they were overjoyed to see it. ¹⁴ The cart came to the field of Joshua of Beth-shemesh and stopped there near a large rock. The people of the city chopped up the cart and offered the cows as a burnt offering to the LORD. ¹⁵ The Levites removed the ark of the LORD, along with the box containing the gold objects, and placed them on the large rock. That day the people of Beth-she-mesh offered burnt offerings and made sacrifices to the LORD. ¹⁶ When the five Philistine rulers observed this, they returned to Ekron that same day.

¹⁷ As a guilt offering to the LORD, the Philistines had sent back one gold tumor for each city: Ashdod, Gaza, Ashkelon, Gath, and Ekron. ¹⁸ The number of gold mice also corresponded to the number of Philistine cities of the five rulers, the fortified cities and the outlying villages. The large rock on which the ark of the LORD was placed is still in the field of Joshua of Beth-she-mesh today.

¹⁹ God struck down the people of Beth-shemesh because they looked inside the ark of the LORD. He struck down seventy persons. The people mourned because the LORD struck them with a great slaughter. ²⁰ The people of Beth-shemesh asked, "Who is able to stand in the presence of the LORD this holy God? To whom should the ark go from here?"

²¹ They sent messengers to the residents of Kiriath-jearim, saying, "The Philistines have returned the ark of the LORD. Come down and get it."

7 So the people of Kiriath-jearim came for the ark of the LORD and took it to Abinadab's house on the hill. They consecrated his son Eleazar to take care of it.

Victory at Mizpah

² Time went by until twenty years had passed since the ark had been taken to Kiriath-jearim. Then the whole house of Israel longed for the LORD. ³ Samuel told them, "If you are returning to the LORD with all your heart, get rid of the foreign gods and the Ashtoreths that are among you, set your hearts on the LORD, and worship only him. Then he will rescue you from the Philistines." ⁴ So the Israelites removed the Baals and the Ashtoreths and only worshiped the LORD.

⁵ Samuel said, "Gather all Israel at Mizpah, and I will pray to the LORD on your behalf." ⁶ When they gathered at Mizpah, they drew water and poured it out in the LORD's presence. They fasted that day, and there they confessed, "We have sinned against the LORD." And Samuel judged the Israelites at Mizpah.

⁷ When the Philistines heard that the Israelites had gathered at Mizpah, their rulers marched up toward Israel. When the Israelites heard about it, they were afraid because of the Philistines. ⁸ The Israelites said to Samuel, "Don't stop crying out to the LORD our God for us, so that he will save us from the Philistines."

⁹ Then Samuel took a young lamb and offered it as a whole burnt offering to the LORD. He cried out to the LORD on behalf of Israel, and the LORD answered him. ¹⁰ Samuel was offering the burnt offering as the Philistines approached to fight against Israel. The LORD thundered loudly against the Philistines that day and threw them into such confusion that they were defeated by Israel. ¹¹ Then the men of Israel charged out of Mizpah and pursued the Philistines striking them down all the way to a place below Beth-car.

¹² Afterward, Samuel took a stone and set it upright between Mizpah and Shen. He named it Ebenezer, explaining, "The LORD has helped us to this point." ¹³ So the Philistines were subdued and did not invade Israel's territory again. The LORD's hand was against the Philistines all of Samuel's life. ¹⁴ The cities from Ekron to Gath, which they had taken from Israel, were restored; Israel even rescued their surrounding territories from Philistine control. There was also peace between Israel and the Amorites.

¹⁵ Samuel judged Israel throughout his life. ¹⁶ Every year he would go on a circuit to Bethel, Gilgal, and Mizpah and would judge Israel at all these locations. ¹⁷ Then he would return to Ramah because his home was there, he judged Israel there, and he built an altar to the LORD there.

Israel's Demand for a King

8 When Samuel grew old, he appointed his sons as judges over Israel. ² His firstborn son's name was Joel and his second was Abijah. They were judges in Beer-sheba. ³ However, his sons did not walk in his ways — they turned toward dishonest profit, took bribes, and perverted justice.

⁴ So all the elders of Israel gathered together and went to Samuel at Ramah. ⁵ They said to him, "Look, you are old, and your sons do not walk in your ways. Therefore, appoint a king to judge us the same as all the other nations have."

⁶ When they said, "Give us a king to judge us," Samuel considered their demand wrong, so he prayed to the LORD. ⁷ But the LORD told him, "Listen to the people and everything they say to you. They have not rejected you; they have rejected me as their king. ⁸ They are doing the same thing to you that they have done to me, since the day I brought them out of Egypt until this day, abandoning me and worshiping other gods. ⁹ Listen to them, but solemnly warn them and tell them about the customary rights of the king who will reign over them."

Israel's demand for a King

When samuel grew old he appointed his son's as juges over is rael. 2 His First born son's name was Joel and his second was gopJan. they were Juges in beer-Sheba. 3 However, his sons did not walk in his ways — they turned toward dishonest Profit, took bribes, and Perverted Justice. 4 So all the elders of Israel gathered together and went to samuel at Ramah. 5 they said to him "Look you are old and your sons do not walk in your ways. there Fore appoint a king to judge us the same as all the other nations have." 6 when they said "give us a king to judge us "samuel considered their demand wrong so he prayed to the lord. 7 but the Lord told them "Listen to the people and everything they say to you. they Have not Rejected you. they Have resected me as their king.

barnabas.

murderer

¹⁰ Samuel told all the LORD's words to the people who were asking him for a king. ¹¹ He said, "These are the rights of the king who will reign over you: He will take your sons and put them to his use in his chariots, on his horses, or running in front of his chariots. ¹² He can appoint them for his use as commanders of thousands or commanders of fifties, to plow his ground and reap his harvest, or to make his weapons of war and the equipment for his chariots. ¹³ He can take your daughters to become perfumers, cooks, and bakers. ¹⁴ He can take your best fields, vineyards, and olive orchards and give them to his servants. ¹⁵ He can take a tenth of your grain and your vineyards and give them to his officials and servants. ¹⁶ He can take your male servants, your female servants, your best cattle, and your donkeys and use them for his work. ¹⁷ He can take a tenth of your flocks, and you yourselves can become his servants. ¹⁸ When that day comes, you will cry out because of the king you've chosen for yourselves, but the LORD won't answer you on that day."

¹⁹ The people refused to listen to Samuel. "No!" they said. "We must have a king over us. ²⁰ Then we'll be like all the other nations: our king will judge us, go out before us, and fight our battles."

²¹ Samuel listened to all the people's words and then repeated them to the LORD. ²² "Listen to them," the LORD told Samuel. "Appoint a king for them."

Then Samuel told the men of Israel, "Each of you, go back to your city."

Saul Anointed King

9 There was a prominent man of Benjamin named Kish son of Abiel, son of Zeror, son of Becorath, son of Aphiah, son of a Benjaminite. ² He had a son named Saul, an impressive young man. There was no one more impressive among the Israelites than he. He stood a head taller than anyone else.

³ One day the donkeys of Saul's father Kish wandered off. Kish said to his son Saul, "Take one of the servants with you and go look for the donkeys." ⁴ Saul and his servant went through the hill country of Ephraim and then through the region of Shalishah, but they didn't find them. They went through the region of Shaalim — nothing. Then they went through the Benjaminite region but still didn't find them.

⁵ When they came to the land of Zuph, Saul said to the servant who was with him, "Come on, let's go back, or my father will stop worrying about the donkeys and start worrying about us."

⁶ "Look," the servant said, "there's a man of God in this city who is highly respected; everything he says is sure to come true. Let's go there now. Maybe he'll tell us which way we should go."

⁷ "Suppose we do go," Saul said to his servant, "what do we take the man? The food from our packs is gone, and there's no gift to take to the man of God. What do we have?"

⁸ The servant answered Saul, "Here, I have a little silver. I'll give it to the man of God, and he will tell us which way we should go."

⁹ Formerly in Israel, a man who was going to inquire of God would say, "Come, let's go to the seer," for the prophet of today was formerly called the seer.

¹⁰ "Good," Saul replied to his servant. "Come on, let's go." So they went to the city where the man of God was. ¹¹ As they were climbing the hill to the city, they found some young women coming out to draw water and asked, "Is the seer here?"

¹² The women answered, "Yes, he is ahead of you. Hurry, he just now entered the city, because there's a sacrifice for the people at the high place today. ¹³ As soon as you enter the city, you will find him before he goes to the high place to eat. The people won't eat until he comes because he must bless the sacrifice; after that, the guests can eat. Go up immediately — you can find him now." ¹⁴ So they went up toward the city.

Saul and his servant were entering the city when they saw Samuel coming toward them on his way to the high place. ¹⁵ Now the day before Saul's arrival, the LORD had informed Samuel, ¹⁶ "At this time tomorrow I will send you a man from the land of Benjamin. Anoint him ruler over my people Israel. He will save them from the Philistines because I have seen the affliction of my people, for their cry has come to me." ¹⁷ When Samuel saw Saul, the LORD told him, "Here is the man I told you about; he will govern my people."

¹⁸ Saul approached Samuel in the city gate and asked, "Would you please tell me where the seer's house is?"

¹⁹ "I am the seer," Samuel answered. "Go up ahead of me to the high place and eat with me today. When I send you off in the morning, I'll tell you everything that's in your heart. ²⁰ As for the donkeys that wandered away from you three days ago, don't worry about them because they've been found. And who does all Israel desire but you and all your father's family?"

²¹ Saul responded, "Am I not a Benjaminite from the smallest of Israel's tribes and isn't my clan the least important of all the clans of the Benjaminite tribe? So why have you said something like this to me?"

²² Samuel took Saul and his servant, brought them to the banquet hall, and gave them a place at the head of the thirty or so men who had been invited. ²³ Then Samuel said to the cook, "Get the portion of meat that I gave you and told you to set aside."

²⁴ The cook picked up the thigh and what was attached to it and set it before Saul. Then Samuel said, "Notice that the reserved piece is set before you. Eat it because it was saved for you for this solemn event at the time I said, 'I've invited the people.'" So Saul ate with Samuel that day. ²⁵ Afterward, they went down from the high place to the city, and Samuel spoke with Saul on the roof.

²⁶ They got up early, and just before dawn, Samuel called to Saul on the roof, "Get up, and I'll send you on your way!" Saul got up, and both he and Samuel went outside. ²⁷ As they were going down to the edge of the city, Samuel said to Saul, "Tell the servant to go on ahead of us, but you stay for a while, and I'll reveal the word of God to you." So the servant went on.

10 Samuel took the flask of oil, poured it out on Saul's head, kissed him, and said, "Hasn't the LORD anointed you ruler over his inheritance? ² Today when you leave me, you'll find two men at Rachel's Grave at Zelzah in the territory of Benjamin. They will say to you, 'The donkeys you went looking for have been found, and now your father has stopped being concerned about the donkeys and is worried about you, asking: What should I do about my son?'

³ "You will proceed from there until you come to the oak of Tabor. Three men going up to God at Bethel will meet you there, one bringing three goats, one bringing three loaves of bread, and one bringing a clay jar of wine. ⁴ They will ask how you are and give you two loaves of bread, which you will accept from them.

⁵ "After that you will come to Gibeah of God where there are Philistine garrisons. When you arrive at the city, you will meet a group of prophets coming down from the high place prophesying. They will be preceded by harps, tambourines, flutes, and lyres. ⁶ The Spirit of the LORD will come powerfully on you, you will prophesy with them, and you will be transformed. ⁷ When these signs have happened to you, do whatever your circumstances require because God is with you. ⁸ Afterward, go ahead of me to Gilgal. I will come to you to offer burnt offerings and to sacrifice fellowship offerings. Wait seven days until I come to you and show you what to do."

⁹ When Saul turned to leave Samuel, God changed his heart, and all the signs came about that day. ¹⁰ When Saul and his

servant arrived at Gibeah, a group of prophets met him. Then the Spirit of God came powerfully on him, and he prophesied along with them.

¹¹ Everyone who knew him previously and saw him prophesy with the prophets asked each other, "What has happened to the son of Kish? Is Saul also among the prophets?"

¹² Then a man who was from there asked, "And who is their father?"

As a result, "Is Saul also among the prophets?" became a popular saying. ¹³ Then Saul finished prophesying and went to the high place.

¹⁴ Saul's uncle asked him and his servant, "Where did you go?"

"To look for the donkeys," Saul answered. "When we saw they weren't there, we went to Samuel."

¹⁵ "Tell me," Saul's uncle asked, "what did Samuel say to you?"

¹⁶ Saul told him, "He assured us the donkeys had been found." However, Saul did not tell him what Samuel had said about the matter of kingship.

Saul Received as King

¹⁷ Samuel summoned the people to the Lord at Mizpah ¹⁸ and said to the Israelites, "This is what the Lord, the God of Israel, says: 'I brought Israel out of Egypt, and I rescued you from the power of the Egyptians and all the kingdoms that were oppressing you.' ¹⁹ But today you have rejected your God, who saves you from all your troubles and afflictions. You said to him, 'You must set a king over us.' Now therefore present yourselves before the Lord by your tribes and clans."

²⁰ Samuel had all the tribes of Israel come forward, and the tribe of Benjamin was selected. ²¹ Then he had the tribe of Benjamin come forward by its clans, and the Matrite clan was selected. Finally, Saul son of Kish was selected. But when they

searched for him, they could not find him. ²²They again inquired of the LORD, "Has the man come here yet?"

The LORD replied, "There he is, hidden among the supplies."

²³They ran and got him from there. When he stood among the people, he stood a head taller than anyone else. ²⁴Samuel said to all the people, "Do you see the one the LORD has chosen? There is no one like him among the entire population."

And all the people shouted, "Long live the king!"

²⁵Samuel proclaimed to the people the rights of kingship. He wrote them on a scroll, which he placed in the presence of the LORD. Then Samuel sent all the people home.

²⁶Saul also went to his home in Gibeah, and brave men whose hearts God had touched went with him. ²⁷But some wicked men said, "How can this guy save us?" They despised him and did not bring him a gift, but Saul said nothing.

Saul's Deliverance of Jabesh-gilead

11 Nahash the Ammonite came up and laid siege to Jabesh-gilead. All the men of Jabesh said to him, "Make a treaty with us, and we will serve you."

²Nahash the Ammonite replied, "I'll make one with you on this condition: that I gouge out everyone's right eye and humiliate all Israel."

³"Don't do anything to us for seven days," the elders of Jabesh said to him, "and let us send messengers throughout the territory of Israel. If no one saves us, we will surrender to you."

⁴When the messengers came to Gibeah, Saul's hometown, and told the terms to the people, all wept aloud. ⁵Just then Saul was coming in from the field behind his oxen. "What's the matter with the people? Why are they weeping?" Saul inquired, and they repeated to him the words of the men from Jabesh.

⁶When Saul heard these words, the Spirit of God suddenly came powerfully on him, and his anger burned furiously. ⁷He

took a team of oxen, cut them in pieces, and sent them throughout the territory of Israel by messengers who said, "This is what will be done to the ox of anyone who doesn't march behind Saul and Samuel." As a result, the terror of the LORD fell on the people, and they went out united.

⁸ Saul counted them at Bezek. There were three hundred thousand Israelites and thirty thousand men from Judah. ⁹ He told the messengers who had come, "Tell this to the men of Jabesh-gilead: 'Deliverance will be yours tomorrow by the time the sun is hot.'" So the messengers told the men of Jabesh, and they rejoiced.

¹⁰ Then the men of Jabesh said to Nahash, "Tomorrow we will come out, and you can do whatever you want to us."

¹¹ The next day Saul organized the troops into three divisions. During the morning watch, they invaded the Ammonite camp and slaughtered them until the heat of the day. There were survivors, but they were so scattered that no two of them were left together.

Saul's Confirmation as King

¹² Afterward, the people said to Samuel, "Who said that Saul should not reign over us? Give us those men so we can kill them!"

¹³ But Saul ordered, "No one will be executed this day, for today the LORD has provided deliverance in Israel."

¹⁴ Then Samuel said to the people, "Come, let's go to Gilgal, so we can renew the kingship there." ¹⁵ So all the people went to Gilgal, and there in the LORD's presence they made Saul king. There they sacrificed fellowship offerings in the LORD's presence, and Saul and all the men of Israel rejoiced greatly.

Samuel's Final Public Speech

12 Then Samuel said to all Israel, "I have carefully listened to everything you said to me and placed a king over you.

²Now you can see that the king is leading you. As for me, I'm old and gray, and my sons are here with you. I have led you from my youth until now. ³Here I am. Bring charges against me before the LORD and his anointed: Whose ox or donkey have I taken? Who have I wronged or mistreated? Who gave me a bribe to overlook something? I will return it to you."

⁴"You haven't wronged us, you haven't mistreated us, and you haven't taken anything from anyone," they responded.

⁵He said to them, "The LORD is a witness against you, and his anointed is a witness today that you haven't found anything in my hand."

"He is a witness," they said.

⁶Then Samuel said to the people, "The LORD, who appointed Moses and Aaron and who brought your ancestors up from the land of Egypt, is a witness. ⁷Now present yourselves, so I may confront you before the LORD about all the righteous acts he has done for you and your ancestors.

⁸"When Jacob went to Egypt, your ancestors cried out to the LORD, and he sent them Moses and Aaron, who led your ancestors out of Egypt and settled them in this place. ⁹But they forgot the LORD their God, so he handed them over to Sisera commander of the army of Hazor, to the Philistines, and to the king of Moab. These enemies fought against them. ¹⁰Then they cried out to the LORD and said, 'We have sinned, for we abandoned the LORD and worshiped the Baals and the Ashtoreths. Now rescue us from the power of our enemies, and we will serve you.' ¹¹So the LORD sent Jerubbaal, Barak, Jephthah, and Samuel. He rescued you from the power of the enemies around you, and you lived securely. ¹²But when you saw that Nahash king of the Ammonites was coming against you, you said to me, 'No, we must have a king reign over us' — even though the LORD your God is your king.

¹³"Now here is the king you've chosen, the one you requested. Look, this is the king the LORD has placed over you. ¹⁴If you fear

the Lord, worship and obey him, and if you don't rebel against the Lord's command, then both you and the king who reigns over you will follow the Lord your God. ¹⁵ However, if you disobey the Lord and rebel against his command, the Lord's hand will be against you as it was against your ancestors.

¹⁶ "Now, therefore, present yourselves and see this great thing that the Lord will do before your eyes. ¹⁷ Isn't the wheat harvest today? I will call on the Lord, and he will send thunder and rain so that you will recognize what an immense evil you committed in the Lord's sight by requesting a king for yourselves." ¹⁸ Samuel called on the Lord, and on that day the Lord sent thunder and rain. As a result, all the people greatly feared the Lord and Samuel.

¹⁹ They pleaded with Samuel, "Pray to the Lord your God for your servants so we won't die! For we have added to all our sins the evil of requesting a king for ourselves."

²⁰ Samuel replied, "Don't be afraid. Even though you have committed all this evil, don't turn away from following the Lord. Instead, worship the Lord with all your heart. ²¹ Don't turn away to follow worthless things that can't profit or rescue you; they are worthless. ²² The Lord will not abandon his people, because of his great name and because he has determined to make you his own people.

²³ "As for me, I vow that I will not sin against the Lord by ceasing to pray for you. I will teach you the good and right way. ²⁴ Above all, fear the Lord and worship him faithfully with all your heart; consider the great things he has done for you. ²⁵ However, if you continue to do what is evil, both you and your king will be swept away."

Saul's Failure

13 Saul was thirty years old when he became king, and he reigned forty-two years over Israel. ² He chose three thousand men from Israel for himself: two thousand were

with Saul at Michmash and in Bethel's hill country, and one thousand were with Jonathan in Gibeah of Benjamin. He sent the rest of the troops away, each to his own tent.

³ Jonathan attacked the Philistine garrison in Gibeah, and the Philistines heard about it. So Saul blew the ram's horn throughout the land saying, "Let the Hebrews hear!" ⁴ And all Israel heard the news, "Saul has attacked the Philistine garrison, and Israel is now repulsive to the Philistines." Then the troops were summoned to join Saul at Gilgal.

⁵ The Philistines also gathered to fight against Israel: three thousand chariots, six thousand horsemen, and troops as numerous as the sand on the seashore. They went up and camped at Michmash, east of Beth-aven.

⁶ The men of Israel saw that they were in trouble because the troops were in a difficult situation. They hid in caves, in thickets, among rocks, and in holes and cisterns. ⁷ Some Hebrews even crossed the Jordan to the land of Gad and Gilead.

Saul, however, was still at Gilgal, and all his troops were gripped with fear. ⁸ He waited seven days for the appointed time that Samuel had set, but Samuel didn't come to Gilgal, and the troops were deserting him. ⁹ So Saul said, "Bring me the burnt offering and the fellowship offerings." Then he offered the burnt offering.

¹⁰ Just as he finished offering the burnt offering, Samuel arrived. So Saul went out to greet him, ¹¹ and Samuel asked, "What have you done?"

Saul answered, "When I saw that the troops were deserting me and you didn't come within the appointed days and the Philistines were gathering at Michmash, ¹² I thought, 'The Philistines will now descend on me at Gilgal, and I haven't sought the LORD's favor.' So I forced myself to offer the burnt offering."

¹³ Samuel said to Saul, "You have been foolish. You have not kept the command the LORD your God gave you. It was at this time that the LORD would have permanently established your

reign over Israel, ¹⁴but now your reign will not endure. The Lord has found a man after his own heart, and the Lord has appointed him as ruler over his people, because you have not done what the Lord commanded." ¹⁵Then Samuel went from Gilgal to Gibeah in Benjamin. Saul registered the troops who were with him, about six hundred men.

¹⁶ Saul, his son Jonathan, and the troops who were with them were staying in Geba of Benjamin, and the Philistines were camped at Michmash. ¹⁷Raiding parties went out from the Philistine camp in three divisions. One division headed toward the Ophrah road leading to the land of Shual. ¹⁸The next division headed toward the Beth-horon road, and the last division headed down the border road that looks out over the Zeboim Valley toward the wilderness.

¹⁹No blacksmith could be found in all the land of Israel because the Philistines had said, "Otherwise, the Hebrews will make swords or spears." ²⁰So all the Israelites went to the Philistines to sharpen their plows, mattocks, axes, and sickles. ²¹The price was two-thirds of a shekel for plows and mattocks, and one-third of a shekel for pitchforks and axes, and for putting a point on a cattle prod. ²²So on the day of battle not a sword or spear could be found in the hand of any of the troops who were with Saul and Jonathan; only Saul and his son Jonathan had weapons.

Jonathan's Victory over the Philistines

²³Now a Philistine garrison took control of the pass at Michmash. **14** ¹That same day Saul's son Jonathan said to the attendant who carried his weapons, "Come on, let's cross over to the Philistine garrison on the other side." However, he did not tell his father.

² Saul was staying under the pomegranate tree in Migron on the outskirts of Gibeah. The troops with him numbered about six hundred. ³ Ahijah, who was wearing an ephod, was also

there. He was the son of Ahitub, the brother of Ichabod son of Phinehas, son of Eli the LORD's priest at Shiloh. But the troops did not know that Jonathan had left.

⁴ There were sharp columns of rock on both sides of the pass that Jonathan intended to cross to reach the Philistine garrison. One was named Bozez and the other Seneh; ⁵ one stood to the north in front of Michmash and the other to the south in front of Geba. ⁶ Jonathan said to the attendant who carried his weapons, "Come on, let's cross over to the garrison of these uncircumcised men. Perhaps the LORD will help us. Nothing can keep the LORD from saving, whether by many or by few."

⁷ His armor-bearer responded, "Do what is in your heart. Go ahead! I'm completely with you."

⁸ "All right," Jonathan replied, "we'll cross over to the men and then let them see us. ⁹ If they say, 'Wait until we reach you,' then we will stay where we are and not go up to them. ¹⁰ But if they say, 'Come on up,' then we'll go up, because the LORD has handed them over to us — that will be our sign."

¹¹ They let themselves be seen by the Philistine garrison, and the Philistines said, "Look, the Hebrews are coming out of the holes where they've been hiding!" ¹² The men of the garrison called to Jonathan and his armor-bearer. "Come on up, and we'll teach you a lesson!" they said.

"Follow me," Jonathan told his armor-bearer, "for the LORD has handed them over to Israel." ¹³ Jonathan climbed up using his hands and feet, with his armor-bearer behind him. Jonathan cut them down, and his armor-bearer followed and finished them off. ¹⁴ In that first assault Jonathan and his armor-bearer struck down about twenty men in a half-acre field.

A Defeat for the Philistines
¹⁵ Terror spread through the Philistine camp and the open fields to all the troops. Even the garrison and the raiding parties were

terrified. The earth shook, and terror spread from God. **¹⁶** When Saul's watchmen in Gibeah of Benjamin looked, they saw the panicking troops scattering in every direction. **¹⁷** So Saul said to the troops with him, "Call the roll and determine who has left us." They called the roll and saw that Jonathan and his armor-bearer were gone.

¹⁸ Saul told Ahijah, "Bring the ark of God," for it was with the Israelites at that time. **¹⁹** While Saul spoke to the priest, the panic in the Philistine camp increased in intensity. So Saul said to the priest, "Stop what you're doing."

²⁰ Saul and all the troops with him assembled and marched to the battle, and there the Philistines were, fighting against each other in great confusion! **²¹** There were Hebrews from the area who had gone earlier into the camp to join the Philistines, but even they joined the Israelites who were with Saul and Jonathan. **²²** When all the Israelite men who had been hiding in the hill country of Ephraim heard that the Philistines were fleeing, they also joined Saul and Jonathan in the battle. **²³** So the LORD saved Israel that day.

Saul's Rash Oath

The battle extended beyond Beth-aven, **²⁴** and the men of Israel were worn out that day, for Saul had placed the troops under an oath: "The man who eats food before evening, before I have taken vengeance on my enemies is cursed." So none of the troops tasted any food.

²⁵ Everyone went into the forest, and there was honey on the ground. **²⁶** When the troops entered the forest, they saw the flow of honey, but none of them ate any of it because they feared the oath. **²⁷** However, Jonathan had not heard his father make the troops swear the oath. He reached out with the end of the staff he was carrying and dipped it into the honeycomb. When he ate the honey, he had renewed energy. **²⁸** Then one of

the troops said, "Your father made the troops solemnly swear, 'The man who eats food today is cursed,' and the troops are exhausted."

²⁹ Jonathan replied, "My father has brought trouble to the land. Just look at how I have renewed energy because I tasted a little of this honey. ³⁰ How much better if the troops had eaten freely today from the plunder they took from their enemies! Then the slaughter of the Philistines would have been much greater."

³¹ The Israelites struck down the Philistines that day from Michmash all the way to Aijalon. Since the Israelites were completely exhausted, ³² they rushed to the plunder, took sheep, goats, cattle, and calves, slaughtered them on the ground, and ate meat with the blood still in it. ³³ Some reported to Saul, "Look, the troops are sinning against the LORD by eating meat with the blood still in it."

Saul said, "You have been unfaithful. Roll a large stone over here at once." ³⁴ He then said, "Go among the troops and say to them, 'Let each man bring me his ox or his sheep. Do the slaughtering here and then you can eat. Don't sin against the LORD by eating meat with the blood in it.'" So every one of the troops brought his ox that night and slaughtered it there. ³⁵ Then Saul built an altar to the LORD; it was the first time he had built an altar to the LORD.

³⁶ Saul said, "Let's go down after the Philistines tonight and plunder them until morning. Don't let even one remain!"

"Do whatever you want," the troops replied.

But the priest said, "Let's approach God here."

³⁷ So Saul inquired of God, "Should I go after the Philistines? Will you hand them over to Israel?" But God did not answer him that day.

³⁸ Saul said, "All you leaders of the troops, come here. Let's investigate how this sin has occurred today. ³⁹ As surely as the

LORD lives who saves Israel, even if it is because of my son Jonathan, he must die!" Not one of the troops answered him.

40 So he said to all Israel, "You will be on one side, and I and my son Jonathan will be on the other side."

And the troops replied, "Do whatever you want."

41 So Saul said to the LORD, "God of Israel, why have you not answered your servant today? If the unrighteousness is in me or in my son Jonathan, LORD God of Israel, give Urim; but if the fault is in your people Israel, give Thummim." Jonathan and Saul were selected, and the troops were cleared of the charge.

42 Then Saul said, "Cast the lot between me and my son Jonathan," and Jonathan was selected. **43** Saul commanded him, "Tell me what you did."

Jonathan told him, "I tasted a little honey with the end of the staff I was carrying. I am ready to die!"

44 Saul declared to him, "May God punish me and do so severely if you do not die, Jonathan!"

45 But the people said to Saul, "Must Jonathan die? He accomplished such a great deliverance for Israel! No, as the LORD lives, not a hair of his head will fall to the ground, for he worked with God's help today." So the people redeemed Jonathan, and he did not die. **46** Then Saul gave up the pursuit of the Philistines, and the Philistines returned to their own territory.

Summary of Saul's Kingship

47 When Saul assumed the kingship over Israel, he fought against all his enemies in every direction: against Moab, the Ammonites, Edom, the kings of Zobah, and the Philistines. Wherever he turned, he caused havoc. **48** He fought bravely, defeated the Amalekites, and rescued Israel from those who plundered them.

49 Saul's sons were Jonathan, Ishvi, and Malchishua. The names of his two daughters were Merab, his firstborn, and

Michal, the younger. ⁵⁰ The name of Saul's wife was Ahinoam daughter of Ahimaaz. The name of the commander of his army was Abner son of Saul's uncle Ner. ⁵¹ Saul's father was Kish. Abner's father was Ner son of Abiel.

⁵² The conflict with the Philistines was fierce all of Saul's days, so whenever Saul noticed any strong or valiant man, he enlisted him.

Saul Rejected as King

15 Samuel told Saul, "The LORD sent me to anoint you as king over his people Israel. Now, listen to the words of the LORD. ² This is what the LORD of Armies says: 'I witnessed what the Amalekites did to the Israelites when they opposed them along the way as they were coming out of Egypt. ³ Now go and attack the Amalekites and completely destroy everything they have. Do not spare them. Kill men and women, infants and nursing babies, oxen and sheep, camels and donkeys.'"

⁴ Then Saul summoned the troops and counted them at Telaim: two hundred thousand foot soldiers and ten thousand men from Judah. ⁵ Saul came to the city of Amalek and set up an ambush in the wadi. ⁶ He warned the Kenites, "Since you showed kindness to all the Israelites when they came out of Egypt, go on and leave! Get away from the Amalekites, or I'll sweep you away with them." So the Kenites withdrew from the Amalekites.

⁷ Then Saul struck down the Amalekites from Havilah all the way to Shur, which is next to Egypt. ⁸ He captured King Agag of Amalek alive, but he completely destroyed all the rest of the people with the sword. ⁹ Saul and the troops spared Agag, and the best of the sheep, goats, cattle, and choice animals, as well as the young rams and the best of everything else. They were not willing to destroy them, but they did destroy all the worthless and unwanted things.

¹⁰ Then the word of the LORD came to Samuel, ¹¹ "I regret that I made Saul king, for he has turned away from following me and has not carried out my instructions." So Samuel became angry and cried out to the LORD all night.

¹² Early in the morning Samuel got up to confront Saul, but it was reported to Samuel, "Saul went to Carmel where he set up a monument for himself. Then he turned around and went down to Gilgal." ¹³ When Samuel came to him, Saul said, "May the LORD bless you. I have carried out the LORD's instructions."

¹⁴ Samuel replied, "Then what is this sound of sheep, goats, and cattle I hear?"

¹⁵ Saul answered, "The troops brought them from the Amalekites and spared the best sheep, goats, and cattle in order to offer a sacrifice to the LORD your God, but the rest we destroyed."

¹⁶ "Stop!" exclaimed Samuel. "Let me tell you what the LORD said to me last night."

"Tell me," he replied.

¹⁷ Samuel continued, "Although you once considered yourself unimportant, haven't you become the leader of the tribes of Israel? The LORD anointed you king over Israel ¹⁸ and then sent you on a mission and said, 'Go and completely destroy the sinful Amalekites. Fight against them until you have annihilated them.' ¹⁹ So why didn't you obey the LORD? Why did you rush on the plunder and do what was evil in the LORD's sight?"

²⁰ "But I did obey the LORD!" Saul answered. "I went on the mission the LORD gave me: I brought back King Agag of Amalek, and I completely destroyed the Amalekites. ²¹ The troops took sheep, goats, and cattle from the plunder — the best of what was set apart for destruction — to sacrifice to the LORD your God at Gilgal."

²² Then Samuel said:

Does the LORD take pleasure in burnt offerings and sacrifices
as much as in obeying the LORD?

Look: to obey is better than sacrifice,
to pay attention is better than the fat of rams.
23 For rebellion is like the sin of divination,
and defiance is like wickedness and idolatry.
Because you have rejected the word of the LORD,
he has rejected you as king.

24 Saul answered Samuel, "I have sinned. I have transgressed the LORD's command and your words. Because I was afraid of the people, I obeyed them. 25 Now therefore, please forgive my sin and return with me so I can worship the LORD." 26 Samuel replied to Saul, "I will not return with you. Because you rejected the word of the LORD, the LORD has rejected you from being king over Israel." 27 When Samuel turned to go, Saul grabbed the corner of his robe, and it tore. 28 Samuel said to him, "The LORD has torn the kingship of Israel away from you today and has given it to your neighbor who is better than you. 29 Furthermore, the Eternal One of Israel does not lie or change his mind, for he is not man who changes his mind." 30 Saul said, "I have sinned. Please honor me now before the elders of my people and before Israel. Come back with me so I can bow in worship to the LORD your God." 31 Then Samuel went back, following Saul, and Saul bowed down to the LORD. 32 Samuel said, "Bring me King Agag of Amalek."

Agag came to him trembling, for he thought, "Certainly the bitterness of death has come." 33 Samuel declared:

As your sword has made women childless,
so your mother will be childless
among women.

Then he hacked Agag to pieces before the LORD at Gilgal. 34 Samuel went to Ramah, and Saul went up to his home in Gibeah of Saul. 35 Even to the day of his death, Samuel never

saw Saul again. Samuel mourned for Saul, and the LORD regretted he had made Saul king over Israel.

Samuel Anoints David

16 The LORD said to Samuel, "How long are you going to mourn for Saul, since I have rejected him as king over Israel? Fill your horn with oil and go. I am sending you to Jesse of Bethlehem because I have selected for myself a king from his sons."

² Samuel asked, "How can I go? Saul will hear about it and kill me!"

The LORD answered, "Take a young cow with you and say, 'I have come to sacrifice to the LORD.' ³ Then invite Jesse to the sacrifice, and I will let you know what you are to do. You are to anoint for me the one I indicate to you."

⁴ Samuel did what the LORD directed and went to Bethlehem. When the elders of the town met him, they trembled and asked, "Do you come in peace?"

⁵ "In peace," he replied. "I've come to sacrifice to the LORD. Consecrate yourselves and come with me to the sacrifice." Then he consecrated Jesse and his sons and invited them to the sacrifice. ⁶ When they arrived, Samuel saw Eliab and said, "Certainly the LORD's anointed one is here before him."

⁷ But the LORD said to Samuel, "Do not look at his appearance or his stature because I have rejected him. Humans do not see what the LORD sees, for humans see what is visible, but the LORD sees the heart."

⁸ Jesse called Abinadab and presented him to Samuel. "The LORD hasn't chosen this one either," Samuel said. ⁹ Then Jesse presented Shammah, but Samuel said, "The LORD hasn't chosen this one either." ¹⁰ After Jesse presented seven of his sons to him, Samuel told Jesse, "The LORD hasn't chosen any of these." ¹¹ Samuel asked him, "Are these all the sons you have?"

"There is still the youngest," he answered, "but right now he's tending the sheep." Samuel told Jesse, "Send for him. We won't sit down to eat until he gets here." ¹² So Jesse sent for him. He had beautiful eyes and a healthy, handsome appearance.

Then the LORD said, "Anoint him, for he is the one." ¹³ So Samuel took the horn of oil and anointed him in the presence of his brothers, and the Spirit of the LORD came powerfully on David from that day forward. Then Samuel set out and went to Ramah.

David in Saul's Court

¹⁴ Now the Spirit of the LORD had left Saul, and an evil spirit sent from the LORD began to torment him, ¹⁵ so Saul's servants said to him, "You see that an evil spirit from God is tormenting you. ¹⁶ Let our lord command your servants here in your presence to look for someone who knows how to play the lyre. Whenever the evil spirit from God comes on you, that person can play the lyre, and you will feel better."

¹⁷ Then Saul commanded his servants, "Find me someone who plays well and bring him to me."

¹⁸ One of the young men answered, "I have seen a son of Jesse of Bethlehem who knows how to play the lyre. He is also a valiant man, a warrior, eloquent, handsome, and the LORD is with him."

¹⁹ Then Saul dispatched messengers to Jesse and said, "Send me your son David, who is with the sheep." ²⁰ So Jesse took a donkey loaded with bread, a wineskin, and one young goat and sent them by his son David to Saul. ²¹ When David came to Saul and entered his service, Saul loved him very much, and David became his armor-bearer. ²² Then Saul sent word to Jesse: "Let David remain in my service, for he has found favor with me." ²³ Whenever the spirit from God came on Saul, David would pick up his lyre and play, and Saul would then be relieved, feel better, and the evil spirit would leave him.

David versus Goliath

17 The Philistines gathered their forces for war at Socoh in Judah and camped between Socoh and Azekah in Ephes-dammim. ² Saul and the men of Israel gathered and camped in the Valley of Elah; then they lined up in battle formation to face the Philistines.

³ The Philistines were standing on one hill, and the Israelites were standing on another hill with a ravine between them. ⁴ Then a champion named Goliath, from Gath, came out from the Philistine camp. He was nine feet, nine inches tall ⁵ and wore a bronze helmet and bronze scale armor that weighed one hundred twenty-five pounds. ⁶ There was bronze armor on his shins, and a bronze javelin was slung between his shoulders. ⁷ His spear shaft was like a weaver's beam, and the iron point of his spear weighed fifteen pounds. In addition, a shield-bearer was walking in front of him.

⁸ He stood and shouted to the Israelite battle formations, "Why do you come out to line up in battle formation?" He asked them, "Am I not a Philistine and are you not servants of Saul? Choose one of your men and have him come down against me. ⁹ If he wins in a fight against me and kills me, we will be your servants. But if I win against him and kill him, then you will be our servants and serve us." ¹⁰ Then the Philistine said, "I defy the ranks of Israel today. Send me a man so we can fight each other!" ¹¹ When Saul and all Israel heard these words from the Philistine, they lost their courage and were terrified.

¹² Now David was the son of the Ephrathite from Bethlehem of Judah named Jesse. Jesse had eight sons and during Saul's reign was already an old man. ¹³ Jesse's three oldest sons had followed Saul to the war, and their names were Eliab, the firstborn, Abinadab, the next, and Shammah, the third, ¹⁴ and David was the youngest. The three oldest had followed Saul, ¹⁵ but David kept going back and forth from Saul to tend his father's flock in Bethlehem.

¹⁶ Every morning and evening for forty days the Philistine came forward and took his stand. ¹⁷ One day Jesse had told his son David, "Take this half-bushel of roasted grain along with these ten loaves of bread for your brothers and hurry to their camp. ¹⁸ Also take these ten portions of cheese to the field commander. Check on the well-being of your brothers and bring a confirmation from them. ¹⁹ They are with Saul and all the men of Israel in the Valley of Elah fighting with the Philistines."

²⁰ So David got up early in the morning, left the flock with someone to keep it, loaded up, and set out as Jesse had charged him.

He arrived at the perimeter of the camp as the army was marching out to its battle formation shouting their battle cry. ²¹ Israel and the Philistines lined up in battle formation facing each other. ²² David left his supplies in the care of the quartermaster and ran to the battle line. When he arrived, he asked his brothers how they were. ²³ While he was speaking with them, suddenly the champion named Goliath, the Philistine from Gath, came forward from the Philistine battle line and shouted his usual words, which David heard. ²⁴ When all the Israelite men saw Goliath, they retreated from him terrified.

²⁵ Previously, an Israelite man had declared, "Do you see this man who keeps coming out? He comes to defy Israel. The king will make the man who kills him very rich and will give him his daughter. The king will also make the family of that man's father exempt from paying taxes in Israel."

²⁶ David spoke to the men who were standing with him: "What will be done for the man who kills that Philistine and removes this disgrace from Israel? Just who is this uncircumcised Philistine that he should defy the armies of the living God?"

²⁷ The troops told him about the offer, concluding, "That is what will be done for the man who kills him."

²⁸ David's oldest brother Eliab listened as he spoke to the men, and he became angry with him. "Why did you come down here?" he asked. "Who did you leave those few sheep with in the wilderness? I know your arrogance and your evil heart — you came down to see the battle!"

²⁹ "What have I done now?" protested David. "It was just a question." ³⁰ Then he turned from those beside him to others in front of him and asked about the offer. The people gave him the same answer as before.

³¹ What David said was overheard and reported to Saul, so he had David brought to him. ³² David said to Saul, "Don't let anyone be discouraged by him; your servant will go and fight this Philistine!"

³³ But Saul replied, "You can't go fight this Philistine. You're just a youth, and he's been a warrior since he was young."

³⁴ David answered Saul, "Your servant has been tending his father's sheep. Whenever a lion or a bear came and carried off a lamb from the flock, ³⁵ I went after it, struck it down, and rescued the lamb from its mouth. If it reared up against me, I would grab it by its fur, strike it down, and kill it. ³⁶ Your servant has killed lions and bears; this uncircumcised Philistine will be like one of them, for he has defied the armies of the living God." ³⁷ Then David said, "The LORD who rescued me from the paw of the lion and the paw of the bear will rescue me from the hand of this Philistine."

Saul said to David, "Go, and may the LORD be with you."

³⁸ Then Saul had his own military clothes put on David. He put a bronze helmet on David's head and had him put on armor. ³⁹ David strapped his sword on over the military clothes and tried to walk, but he was not used to them. "I can't walk in these," David said to Saul, "I'm not used to them." So David took them off. ⁴⁰ Instead, he took his staff in his hand and chose five smooth stones from the wadi and put them in the pouch, in his

shepherd's bag. Then, with his sling in his hand, he approached the Philistine.

⁴¹The Philistine came closer and closer to David, with the shield-bearer in front of him. ⁴²When the Philistine looked and saw David, he despised him because he was just a youth, healthy and handsome. ⁴³He said to David, "Am I a dog that you come against me with sticks?" Then he cursed David by his gods. ⁴⁴"Come here," the Philistine called to David, "and I'll give your flesh to the birds of the sky and the wild beasts!"

⁴⁵David said to the Philistine, "You come against me with a sword, spear, and javelin, but I come against you in the name of the Lord of Armies, the God of the ranks of Israel — you have defied him. ⁴⁶Today, the Lord will hand you over to me. Today, I'll strike you down, remove your head, and give the corpses of the Philistine camp to the birds of the sky and the wild creatures of the earth. Then all the world will know that Israel has a God, ⁴⁷and this whole assembly will know that it is not by sword or by spear that the Lord saves, for the battle is the Lord's. He will hand you over to us."

⁴⁸When the Philistine started forward to attack him, David ran quickly to the battle line to meet the Philistine. ⁴⁹David put his hand in the bag, took out a stone, slung it, and hit the Philistine on his forehead. The stone sank into his forehead, and he fell facedown to the ground. ⁵⁰David defeated the Philistine with a sling and a stone. David overpowered the Philistine and killed him without having a sword. ⁵¹David ran and stood over him. He grabbed the Philistine's sword, pulled it from its sheath, and used it to kill him. Then he cut off his head. When the Philistines saw that their hero was dead, they fled. ⁵²The men of Israel and Judah rallied, shouting their battle cry, and chased the Philistines to the entrance of the valley and to the gates of Ekron. Philistine bodies were strewn all along the Shaaraim road to Gath and Ekron.

⁵³ When the Israelites returned from the pursuit of the Philistines, they plundered their camps. ⁵⁴ David took Goliath's head and brought it to Jerusalem, but he put Goliath's weapons in his own tent.

⁵⁵ When Saul had seen David going out to confront the Philistine, he asked Abner the commander of the army, "Whose son is this youth, Abner?"

"Your Majesty, as surely as you live, I don't know," Abner replied.

⁵⁶ The king said, "Find out whose son this young man is!"

⁵⁷ When David returned from killing the Philistine, Abner took him and brought him before Saul with the Philistine's head still in his hand. ⁵⁸ Saul said to him, "Whose son are you, young man?"

"The son of your servant Jesse of Bethlehem," David answered.

David's Success

18 When David had finished speaking with Saul, Jonathan was bound to David in close friendship, and loved him as much as he loved himself. ² Saul kept David with him from that day on and did not let him return to his father's house.

³ Jonathan made a covenant with David because he loved him as much as himself. ⁴ Then Jonathan removed the robe he was wearing and gave it to David, along with his military tunic, his sword, his bow, and his belt.

⁵ David marched out with the army and was successful in everything Saul sent him to do. Saul put him in command of the fighting men, which pleased all the people and Saul's servants as well.

⁶ As the troops were coming back, when David was returning from killing the Philistine, the women came out from all the cities of Israel to meet King Saul, singing and dancing with

tambourines, with shouts of joy, and with three-stringed instruments. [7] As they danced, the women sang:

> Saul has killed his thousands,
> but David his tens of thousands.

[8] Saul was furious and resented this song. "They credited tens of thousands to David," he complained, "but they only credited me with thousands. What more can he have but the kingdom?" [9] So Saul watched David jealously from that day forward.

Saul Attempts to Kill David

[10] The next day an evil spirit sent from God came powerfully on Saul, and he began to rave inside the palace. David was playing the lyre as usual, but Saul was holding a spear, [11] and he threw it, thinking, "I'll pin David to the wall." But David got away from him twice.

[12] Saul was afraid of David, because the LORD was with David but had left Saul. [13] Therefore, Saul sent David away from him and made him commander over a thousand men. David led the troops [14] and continued to be successful in all his activities because the LORD was with him. [15] When Saul observed that David was very successful, he dreaded him. [16] But all Israel and Judah loved David because he was leading their troops. [17] Saul told David, "Here is my oldest daughter Merab. I'll give her to you as a wife if you will be a warrior for me and fight the LORD's battles." But Saul was thinking, "I don't need to raise a hand against him; let the hand of the Philistines be against him."

[18] Then David responded, "Who am I, and what is my family or my father's clan in Israel that I should become the king's son-in-law?" [19] When it was time to give Saul's daughter Merab to David, she was given to Adriel the Meholathite as a wife.

David's Marriage to Michal

²⁰ Now Saul's daughter Michal loved David, and when it was reported to Saul, it pleased him. ²¹ "I'll give her to him," Saul thought. "She'll be a trap for him, and the hand of the Philistines will be against him." So Saul said to David a second time, "You can now be my son-in-law."

²² Saul then ordered his servants, "Speak to David in private and tell him, 'Look, the king is pleased with you, and all his servants love you. Therefore, you should become the king's son-in-law.' "

²³ Saul's servants reported these words directly to David, but he replied, "Is it trivial in your sight to become the king's son-in-law? I am a poor commoner."

²⁴ The servants reported back to Saul, "These are the words David spoke."

²⁵ Then Saul replied, "Say this to David: 'The king desires no other bride-price except a hundred Philistine foreskins, to take revenge on his enemies.' " Actually, Saul intended to cause David's death at the hands of the Philistines.

²⁶ When the servants reported these terms to David, he was pleased to become the king's son-in-law. Before the wedding day arrived, ²⁷ David and his men went out and killed two hundred Philistines. He brought their foreskins and presented them as full payment to the king to become his son-in-law. Then Saul gave his daughter Michal to David as his wife. ²⁸ Saul realized that the LORD was with David and that his daughter Michal loved him, ²⁹ and he became even more afraid of David. As a result, Saul was David's enemy from then on.

³⁰ Every time the Philistine commanders came out to fight, David was more successful than all of Saul's officers. So his name became well known.

David Delivered from Saul

19 Saul ordered his son Jonathan and all his servants to kill David. But Saul's son Jonathan liked David very much, ² so he told him, "My father, Saul, intends to kill you. Be on your guard in the morning and hide in a secret place and stay there. ³ I'll go out and stand beside my father in the field where you are and talk to him about you. When I see what he says, I'll tell you."

⁴ Jonathan spoke well of David to his father, Saul. He said to him, "The king should not sin against his servant David. He hasn't sinned against you; in fact, his actions have been a great advantage to you. ⁵ He took his life in his hands when he struck down the Philistine, and the LORD brought about a great victory for all Israel. You saw it and rejoiced, so why would you sin against innocent blood by killing David for no reason?"

⁶ Saul listened to Jonathan's advice and swore an oath: "As surely as the LORD lives, David will not be killed." ⁷ So Jonathan summoned David and told him all these words. Then Jonathan brought David to Saul, and he served him as he did before.

⁸ When war broke out again, David went out and fought against the Philistines. He defeated them with such great force that they fled from him.

⁹ Now an evil spirit sent from the LORD came on Saul as he was sitting in his palace holding a spear. David was playing the lyre, ¹⁰ and Saul tried to pin David to the wall with the spear. As the spear struck the wall, David eluded Saul, ran away, and escaped that night. ¹¹ Saul sent agents to David's house to watch for him and kill him in the morning. But his wife Michal warned David, "If you don't escape tonight, you will be dead tomorrow!" ¹² So she lowered David from the window, and he fled and escaped. ¹³ Then Michal took the household idol and put it on the bed, placed some goat hair on its head, and covered it with a garment. ¹⁴ When Saul sent agents to seize David, Michal said, "He's sick."

¹⁵ Saul sent the agents back to see David and said, "Bring him on his bed so I can kill him." ¹⁶ When the agents arrived, to their surprise, the household idol was on the bed with some goat hair on its head.

¹⁷ Saul asked Michal, "Why did you deceive me like this? You sent my enemy away, and he has escaped!"

She answered him, "He said to me, 'Let me go! Why should I kill you?'"

¹⁸ So David fled and escaped and went to Samuel at Ramah and told him everything Saul had done to him. Then he and Samuel left and stayed at Naioth.

¹⁹ When it was reported to Saul that David was at Naioth in Ramah, ²⁰ he sent agents to seize David. However, when they saw the group of prophets prophesying with Samuel leading them, the Spirit of God came on Saul's agents, and they also started prophesying. ²¹ When they reported to Saul, he sent other agents, and they also began prophesying. So Saul tried again and sent a third group of agents, and even they began prophesying. ²² Then Saul himself went to Ramah. He came to the large cistern at Secu and asked, "Where are Samuel and David?"

"At Naioth in Ramah," someone said.

²³ So he went to Naioth in Ramah. The Spirit of God also came on him, and as he walked along, he prophesied until he entered Naioth in Ramah. ²⁴ Saul then removed his clothes and also prophesied before Samuel; he collapsed and lay naked all that day and all that night. That is why they say, "Is Saul also among the prophets?"

Jonathan Protects David

20 David fled from Naioth in Ramah and came to Jonathan and asked, "What have I done? What did I do wrong? How have I sinned against your father so that he wants to take my life?"

² Jonathan said to him, "No, you won't die. Listen, my father doesn't do anything, great or small, without telling me. So why would he hide this matter from me? This can't be true."

³ But David said, "Your father certainly knows that I have found favor with you. He has said, 'Jonathan must not know of this, or else he will be grieved.'" David also swore, "As surely as the LORD lives and as you yourself live, there is but a step between me and death."

⁴ Jonathan said to David, "Whatever you say, I will do for you."

⁵ So David told him, "Look, tomorrow is the New Moon, and I'm supposed to sit down and eat with the king. Instead, let me go, and I'll hide in the countryside for the next two nights. ⁶ If your father misses me at all, say, 'David urgently requested my permission to go quickly to his hometown, Bethlehem, for an annual sacrifice there involving the whole clan.' ⁷ If he says, 'Good,' then your servant is safe, but if he becomes angry, you will know he has evil intentions. ⁸ Deal kindly with your servant, for you have brought me into a covenant with you before the LORD. If I have done anything wrong, then kill me yourself; why take me to your father?"

⁹ "No!" Jonathan responded. "If I ever find out my father has evil intentions against you, wouldn't I tell you about it?"

¹⁰ So David asked Jonathan, "Who will tell me if your father answers you harshly?"

¹¹ He answered David, "Come on, let's go out to the countryside." So both of them went out to the countryside. ¹² "By the LORD, the God of Israel, I will sound out my father by this time tomorrow or the next day. If I find out that he is favorable toward you, will I not send for you and tell you? ¹³ If my father intends to bring evil on you, may the LORD punish Jonathan and do so severely if I do not tell you and send you away so you may leave safely. May the LORD be with you, just as he was with my father. ¹⁴ If I continue to live, show me kindness

from the LORD, but if I die, ¹⁵ don't ever withdraw your kindness from my household — not even when the LORD cuts off every one of David's enemies from the face of the earth." ¹⁶ Then Jonathan made a covenant with the house of David, saying, "May the LORD hold David's enemies accountable." ¹⁷ Jonathan once again swore to David in his love for him, because he loved him as he loved himself.

¹⁸ Then Jonathan said to him, "Tomorrow is the New Moon; you'll be missed because your seat will be empty. ¹⁹ The following day hurry down and go to the place where you hid on the day this incident began and stay beside the rock Ezel. ²⁰ I will shoot three arrows beside it as if I'm aiming at a target. ²¹ Then I will send a servant and say, 'Go and find the arrows!' Now, if I expressly say to the servant, 'Look, the arrows are on this side of you — get them,' then come, because as the LORD lives, it is safe for you and there is no problem. ²² But if I say this to the youth, 'Look, the arrows are beyond you!' then go, for the LORD is sending you away. ²³ As for the matter you and I have spoken about, the LORD will be a witness between you and me forever." ²⁴ So David hid in the countryside.

At the New Moon, the king sat down to eat the meal. ²⁵ He sat at his usual place on the seat by the wall. Jonathan sat facing him and Abner took his place beside Saul, but David's place was empty. ²⁶ Saul did not say anything that day because he thought, "Something unexpected has happened; he must be ceremonially unclean — yes, that's it, he is unclean."

²⁷ However, the day after the New Moon, the second day, David's place was still empty, and Saul asked his son Jonathan, "Why didn't Jesse's son come to the meal either yesterday or today?"

²⁸ Jonathan answered, "David asked for my permission to go to Bethlehem. ²⁹ He said, 'Please let me go because our clan is holding a sacrifice in the town, and my brother has told me to

be there. So now, if I have found favor with you, let me go so I can see my brothers.' That's why he didn't come to the king's table."

³⁰ Then Saul became angry with Jonathan and shouted, "You son of a perverse and rebellious woman! Don't I know that you are siding with Jesse's son to your own shame and to the disgrace of your mother? ³¹ Every day Jesse's son lives on earth you and your kingship are not secure. Now send for him and bring him to me — he must die!"

³² Jonathan answered his father back, "Why is he to be killed? What has he done?"

³³ Then Saul threw his spear at Jonathan to kill him, so he knew that his father was determined to kill David. ³⁴ He got up from the table fiercely angry and did not eat any food that second day of the New Moon, for he was grieved because of his father's shameful behavior toward David.

³⁵ In the morning Jonathan went out to the countryside for the appointed meeting with David. A young servant was with him. ³⁶ He said to the servant, "Run and find the arrows I'm shooting." As the servant ran, Jonathan shot an arrow beyond him. ³⁷ He came to the location of the arrow that Jonathan had shot, but Jonathan called to him and said, "The arrow is beyond you, isn't it?" ³⁸ Then Jonathan called to him, "Hurry up and don't stop!" Jonathan's servant picked up the arrow and returned to his master. ³⁹ He did not know anything; only Jonathan and David knew the arrangement. ⁴⁰ Then Jonathan gave his equipment to the servant who was with him and said, "Go, take it back to the city."

⁴¹ When the servant had gone, David got up from the south side of the stone Ezel, fell facedown to the ground, and paid homage three times. Then he and Jonathan kissed each other and wept with each other, though David wept more.

⁴² Jonathan then said to David, "Go in the assurance the two of us pledged in the name of the LORD when we said, 'The LORD

will be a witness between you and me and between my off-spring and your offspring forever.'" Then David left, and Jonathan went into the city.

David Flees to Nob

21 David went to the priest Ahimelech at Nob. Ahimelech was afraid to meet David, so he said to him, "Why are you alone and no one is with you?"

² David answered the priest Ahimelech, "The king gave me a mission, but he told me, 'Don't let anyone know anything about the mission I'm sending you on or what I have ordered you to do.' I have stationed my young men at a certain place. ³ Now what do you have on hand? Give me five loaves of bread or whatever can be found."

⁴ The priest told him, "There is no ordinary bread on hand. However, there is consecrated bread, but the young men may eat it only if they have kept themselves from women."

⁵ David answered him, "I swear that women are being kept from us, as always when I go out to battle. The young men's bodies are consecrated even on an ordinary mission, so of course their bodies are consecrated today." ⁶ So the priest gave him the consecrated bread, for there was no bread there except the Bread of the Presence that had been removed from the presence of the LORD. When the bread was removed, it had been replaced with warm bread.

⁷ One of Saul's servants, detained before the LORD, was there that day. His name was Doeg the Edomite, chief of Saul's shepherds.

⁸ David said to Ahimelech, "Do you have a spear or sword on hand? I didn't even bring my sword or my weapons since the king's mission was urgent."

⁹ The priest replied, "The sword of Goliath the Philistine, whom you killed in the Valley of Elah, is here, wrapped in a

cloth behind the ephod. If you want to take it for yourself, then take it, for there isn't another one here."

"There's none like it!" David said. "Give it to me."

David Flees to Gath

¹⁰ David fled that day from Saul's presence and went to King Achish of Gath. ¹¹ But Achish's servants said to him, "Isn't this David, the king of the land? Don't they sing about him during their dances:

Saul has killed his thousands,
but David his tens of thousands?"

¹² David took this to heart and became very afraid of King Achish of Gath, ¹³ so he pretended to be insane in their presence. He acted like a madman around them, scribbling on the doors of the city gate and letting saliva run down his beard.

¹⁴ "Look! You can see the man is crazy," Achish said to his servants. "Why did you bring him to me? ¹⁵ Do I have such a shortage of crazy people that you brought this one to act crazy around me? Is this one going to come into my house?"

Saul's Increasing Paranoia

22 So David left Gath and took refuge in the cave of Adullam. When David's brothers and his father's whole family heard, they went down and joined him there. ² In addition, every man who was desperate, in debt, or discontented rallied around him, and he became their leader. About four hundred men were with him.

³ From there David went to Mizpeh of Moab where he said to the king of Moab, "Please let my father and mother stay with you until I know what God will do for me." ⁴ So he left them in the care of the king of Moab, and they stayed with him the whole time David was in the stronghold.

⁵ Then the prophet Gad said to David, "Don't stay in the stronghold. Leave and return to the land of Judah." So David left and went to the forest of Hereth.

⁶ Saul heard that David and his men had been discovered. At that time Saul was in Gibeah, sitting under the tamarisk tree at the high place. His spear was in his hand, and all his servants were standing around him. ⁷ Saul said to his servants, "Listen, men of Benjamin: Is Jesse's son going to give all of you fields and vineyards? Do you think he'll make all of you commanders of thousands and commanders of hundreds? ⁸ That's why all of you have conspired against me! Nobody tells me when my own son makes a covenant with Jesse's son. None of you cares about me or tells me that my son has stirred up my own servant to wait in ambush for me, as is the case today."

⁹ Then Doeg the Edomite, who was in charge of Saul's servants, answered, "I saw Jesse's son come to Ahimelech son of Ahitub at Nob. ¹⁰ Ahimelech inquired of the Lᴏʀᴅ for him and gave him provisions. He also gave him the sword of Goliath the Philistine."

Slaughter of the Priests

¹¹ The king sent messengers to summon the priest Ahimelech son of Ahitub, and his father's whole family, who were priests in Nob. All of them came to the king. ¹² Then Saul said, "Listen, son of Ahitub!"

"I'm at your service, my lord," he said.

¹³ Saul asked him, "Why did you and Jesse's son conspire against me? You gave him bread and a sword and inquired of God for him, so he could rise up against me and wait in ambush, as is the case today."

¹⁴ Ahimelech replied to the king, "Who among all your servants is as faithful as David? He is the king's son-in-law, captain of your bodyguard, and honored in your house. ¹⁵ Was today

the first time I inquired of God for him? Of course not! Please don't let the king make an accusation against your servant or any of my father's family, for your servant didn't have any idea about all this."

16 But the king said, "You will die, Ahimelech — you and your father's whole family!"

17 Then the king ordered the guards standing by him, "Turn and kill the priests of the LORD because they sided with David. For they knew he was fleeing, but they didn't tell me." But the king's servants would not lift a hand to execute the priests of the LORD.

18 So the king said to Doeg, "Go and execute the priests!" So Doeg the Edomite went and executed the priests himself. On that day, he killed eighty-five men who wore linen ephods. **19** He also struck down Nob, the city of the priests, with the sword — both men and women, infants and nursing babies, oxen, donkeys, and sheep.

20 However, one of the sons of Ahimelech son of Ahitub escaped. His name was Abiathar, and he fled to David. **21** Abiathar told David that Saul had killed the priests of the LORD. **22** Then David said to Abiathar, "I knew that Doeg the Edomite was there that day and that he was sure to report to Saul. I myself am responsible for the lives of everyone in your father's family. **23** Stay with me. Don't be afraid, for the one who wants to take my life wants to take your life. You will be safe with me."

Deliverance at Keilah

23 It was reported to David, "Look, the Philistines are fighting against Keilah and raiding the threshing floors."

2 So David inquired of the LORD: "Should I launch an attack against these Philistines?"

The LORD answered David, "Launch an attack against the Philistines and rescue Keilah."

³ But David's men said to him, "Look, we're afraid here in Judah; how much more if we go to Keilah against the Philistine forces!"

⁴ Once again, David inquired of the LORD, and the LORD answered him, "Go at once to Keilah, for I will hand the Philistines over to you." ⁵ Then David and his men went to Keilah, fought against the Philistines, drove their livestock away, and inflicted heavy losses on them. So David rescued the inhabitants of Keilah. ⁶ Abiathar son of Ahimelech fled to David at Keilah, and he brought an ephod with him.

⁷ When it was reported to Saul that David had gone to Keilah, he said, "God has handed him over to me, for he has trapped himself by entering a town with barred gates." ⁸ Then Saul summoned all the troops to go to war at Keilah and besiege David and his men.

⁹ When David learned that Saul was plotting evil against him, he said to the priest Abiathar, "Bring the ephod." ¹⁰ Then David said, "LORD God of Israel, your servant has reliable information that Saul intends to come to Keilah and destroy the town because of me. ¹¹ Will the citizens of Keilah hand me over to him? Will Saul come down as your servant has heard? LORD God of Israel, please tell your servant."

The LORD answered, "He will come down."

¹² Then David asked, "Will the citizens of Keilah hand me and my men over to Saul?"

"They will," the LORD responded.

¹³ So David and his men, numbering about six hundred, left Keilah at once and moved from place to place. When it was reported to Saul that David had escaped from Keilah, he called off the expedition. ¹⁴ David then stayed in the wilderness strongholds and in the hill country of the Wilderness of Ziph. Saul searched for him every day, but God did not hand David over to him.

A Renewed Covenant

15 David was in the Wilderness of Ziph in Horesh when he saw that Saul had come out to take his life. **16** Then Saul's son Jonathan came to David in Horesh and encouraged him in his faith in God, **17** saying, "Don't be afraid, for my father Saul will never lay a hand on you. You yourself will be king over Israel, and I'll be your second-in-command. Even my father Saul knows it is true." **18** Then the two of them made a covenant in the LORD's presence. Afterward, David remained in Horesh, while Jonathan went home.

David's Narrow Escape

19 Some Ziphites came up to Saul at Gibeah and said, "Isn't it true that David is hiding among us in the strongholds in Horesh on the hill of Hachilah south of Jeshimon? **20** So now, whenever the king wants to come down, let him come down. As for us, we will be glad to hand him over to the king."

21 "May you be blessed by the LORD," replied Saul, "for you have shown concern for me. **22** Go and check again. Investigate where he goes and who has seen him there; they tell me he is extremely cunning. **23** Investigate all the places where he hides. Then come back to me with accurate information, and I'll go with you. If it turns out he really is in the region, I'll search for him among all the clans of Judah." **24** So they went to Ziph ahead of Saul.

Now David and his men were in the wilderness near Maon in the Arabah south of Jeshimon, **25** and Saul and his men went to look for him. When David was told about it, he went down to the rock and stayed in the Wilderness of Maon. Saul heard of this and pursued David there.

26 Saul went along one side of the mountain and David and his men went along the other side. Even though David was hurrying to get away from Saul, Saul and his men were closing in

on David and his men to capture them. ²⁷ Then a messenger came to Saul saying, "Come quickly, because the Philistines have raided the land!" ²⁸ So Saul broke off his pursuit of David and went to engage the Philistines. Therefore, that place was named the Rock of Separation. ²⁹ From there David went up and stayed in the strongholds of En-gedi.

David Spares Saul

24 When Saul returned from pursuing the Philistines, he was told, "David is in the wilderness near En-gedi." ² So Saul took three thousand of Israel's fit young men and went to look for David and his men in front of the Rocks of the Wild Goats. ³ When Saul came to the sheep pens along the road, a cave was there, and he went in to relieve himself. David and his men were staying in the recesses of the cave, ⁴ so they said to him, "Look, this is the day the LORD told you about: 'I will hand your enemy over to you so you can do to him whatever you desire.'" Then David got up and secretly cut off the corner of Saul's robe.

⁵ Afterward, David's conscience bothered him because he had cut off the corner of Saul's robe. ⁶ He said to his men, "As the Lord is my witness, I would never do such a thing to my lord, the LORD's anointed. I will never lift my hand against him, since he is the LORD's anointed." ⁷ With these words David persuaded his men, and he did not let them rise up against Saul.

Then Saul left the cave and went on his way. ⁸ After that, David got up, went out of the cave, and called to Saul, "My lord the king!" When Saul looked behind him, David knelt low with his face to the ground and paid homage. ⁹ David said to Saul, "Why do you listen to the words of people who say, 'Look, David intends to harm you'? ¹⁰ You can see with your own eyes that the LORD handed you over to me today in the cave. Someone advised me to kill you, but I took pity on you and said: I won't

lift my hand against my lord, since he is the LORD's anointed. ¹¹ Look, my father! Look at the corner of your robe in my hand, for I cut it off, but I didn't kill you. Recognize that I've committed no crime or rebellion. I haven't sinned against you even though you are hunting me down to take my life.

¹² "May the LORD judge between me and you, and may the LORD take vengeance on you for me, but my hand will never be against you. ¹³ As the old proverb says, 'Wickedness comes from wicked people.' My hand will never be against you. ¹⁴ Who has the king of Israel come after? What are you chasing after? A dead dog? A single flea? ¹⁵ May the LORD be judge and decide between you and me. May he take notice and plead my case and deliver me from you."

¹⁶ When David finished saying these things to him, Saul replied, "Is that your voice, David my son?" Then Saul wept aloud ¹⁷ and said to David, "You are more righteous than I, for you have done what is good to me though I have done what is evil to you. ¹⁸ You yourself have told me today what good you did for me: when the LORD handed me over to you, you didn't kill me. ¹⁹ When a man finds his enemy, does he let him go unharmed? May the LORD repay you with good for what you've done for me today.

²⁰ "Now I know for certain you will be king, and the kingdom of Israel will be established in your hand. ²¹ Therefore swear to me by the LORD that you will not cut off my descendants or wipe out my name from my father's family." ²² So David swore to Saul. Then Saul went back home, and David and his men went up to the stronghold.

David, Nabal, and Abigail

25 Samuel died, and all Israel assembled to mourn for him, and they buried him by his home in Ramah. David then went down to the Wilderness of Paran.

² A man in Maon had a business in Carmel; he was a very rich man with three thousand sheep and one thousand goats and was shearing his sheep in Carmel. ³ The man's name was Nabal, and his wife's name, Abigail. The woman was intelligent and beautiful, but the man, a Calebite, was harsh and evil in his dealings.

⁴ While David was in the wilderness, he heard that Nabal was shearing sheep, ⁵ so David sent ten young men instructing them, "Go up to Carmel, and when you come to Nabal, greet him in my name. ⁶ Then say this: 'Long life to you, and peace to you, peace to your family, and peace to all that is yours. ⁷ I hear that you are shearing. When your shepherds were with us, we did not harass them, and nothing of theirs was missing the whole time they were in Carmel. ⁸ Ask your young men, and they will tell you. So let my young men find favor with you, for we have come on a feast day. Please give whatever you have on hand to your servants and to your son David.'"

⁹ David's young men went and said all these things to Nabal on David's behalf, and they waited. ¹⁰ Nabal asked them, "Who is David? Who is Jesse's son? Many slaves these days are running away from their masters. ¹¹ Am I supposed to take my bread, my water, and my meat that I butchered for my shearers and give them to these men? I don't know where they are from."

¹² David's young men retraced their steps. When they returned to him, they reported all these words. ¹³ He said to his men, "All of you, put on your swords!" So each man put on his sword, and David also put on his sword. About four hundred men followed David while two hundred stayed with the supplies.

¹⁴ One of Nabal's young men informed Abigail, Nabal's wife, "Look, David sent messengers from the wilderness to greet our master, but he screamed at them. ¹⁵ The men treated us very

well. When we were in the field, we weren't harassed and nothing of ours was missing the whole time we were living among them. **16** They were a wall around us, both day and night, the entire time we were with them herding the sheep. **17** Now consider carefully what you should do, because there is certain to be trouble for our master and his entire family. He is such a worthless fool nobody can talk to him!"

18 Abigail hurried, taking two hundred loaves of bread, two clay jars of wine, five butchered sheep, a bushel of roasted grain, one hundred clusters of raisins, and two hundred cakes of pressed figs, and loaded them on donkeys. **19** Then she said to her male servants, "Go ahead of me. I will be right behind you." But she did not tell her husband, Nabal.

20 As she rode the donkey down a mountain pass hidden from view, she saw David and his men coming toward her and met them. **21** David had just said, "I guarded everything that belonged to this man in the wilderness for nothing. He was not missing anything, yet he paid me back evil for good. **22** May God punish me and do so severely if I let any of his males survive until morning."

23 When Abigail saw David, she quickly got off the donkey and knelt down with her face to the ground and paid homage to David. **24** She knelt at his feet and said, "The guilt is mine, my lord, but please let your servant speak to you directly. Listen to the words of your servant. **25** My lord should pay no attention to this worthless fool Nabal, for he lives up to his name: His name means 'stupid,' and stupidity is all he knows. I, your servant, didn't see my lord's young men whom you sent. **26** Now my lord, as surely as the LORD lives and as you yourself live— it is the LORD who kept you from participating in bloodshed and avenging yourself by your own hand—may your enemies and those who intend to harm my lord be like Nabal. **27** Let this gift your servant has brought to my lord be given to the young men

who follow my lord. ²⁸ Please forgive your servant's offense, for the LORD is certain to make a lasting dynasty for my lord because he fights the LORD's battles. Throughout your life, may evil not be found in you.

²⁹ "Someone is pursuing you and intends to take your life. My lord's life is tucked safely in the place where the LORD your God protects the living, but he is flinging away your enemies' lives like stones from a sling. ³⁰ When the LORD does for my lord all the good he promised you and appoints you ruler over Israel, ³¹ there will not be remorse or a troubled conscience for my lord because of needless bloodshed or my lord's revenge. And when the LORD does good things for my lord, may you remember me your servant."

³² Then David said to Abigail, "Blessed be the LORD God of Israel, who sent you to meet me today! ³³ May your discernment be blessed, and may you be blessed. Today you kept me from participating in bloodshed and avenging myself by my own hand. ³⁴ Otherwise, as surely as the LORD God of Israel lives, who prevented me from harming you, if you had not come quickly to meet me, Nabal wouldn't have had any males left by morning light." ³⁵ Then David accepted what she had brought him and said, "Go home in peace. See, I have heard what you said and have granted your request."

³⁶ Then Abigail went to Nabal, and there he was in his house, holding a feast fit for a king. Nabal's heart was cheerful, and he was very drunk, so she didn't say anything to him until morning light.

³⁷ In the morning when Nabal sobered up, his wife told him about these events. His heart died and he became a stone. ³⁸ About ten days later, the LORD struck Nabal dead.

³⁹ When David heard that Nabal was dead, he said, "Blessed be the LORD who championed my cause against Nabal's insults and restrained his servant from doing evil. The LORD brought Nabal's evil deeds back on his own head."

Then David sent messengers to speak to Abigail about marrying him. [40] When David's servants came to Abigail at Carmel, they said to her, "David sent us to bring you to him as a wife."

[41] She stood up, paid homage with her face to the ground, and said, "Here I am, your servant, a slave to wash the feet of my lord's servants." [42] Then Abigail got up quickly, and with her five female servants accompanying her, rode on the donkey following David's messengers. And so she became his wife.

[43] David also married Ahinoam of Jezreel, and the two of them became his wives. [44] But Saul gave his daughter Michal, David's wife, to Palti son of Laish, who was from Gallim.

David Again Spares Saul

26 Then the Ziphites came to Saul at Gibeah saying, "David is hiding on the hill of Hachilah opposite Jeshimon." [2] So Saul, accompanied by three thousand of the fit young men of Israel, went immediately to the Wilderness of Ziph to search for David there. [3] Saul camped beside the road at the hill of Hachilah opposite Jeshimon. David was living in the wilderness and discovered Saul had come there after him. [4] So David sent out spies and knew for certain that Saul had come. [5] Immediately, David went to the place where Saul had camped. He saw the place where Saul and Abner son of Ner, the commander of his army, were lying down. Saul was lying inside the inner circle of the camp with the troops camped around him. [6] Then David asked Ahimelech the Hethite and Joab's brother Abishai son of Zeruiah, "Who will go with me into the camp to Saul?"

"I'll go with you," answered Abishai.

[7] That night, David and Abishai came to the troops, and Saul was lying there asleep in the inner circle of the camp with his spear stuck in the ground by his head. Abner and the troops were lying around him. [8] Then Abishai said to David, "Today God has delivered your enemy to you. Let me thrust the spear

through him into the ground just once. I won't have to strike him twice!"

⁹ But David said to Abishai, "Don't destroy him, for who can lift a hand against the LORD's anointed and be innocent?" ¹⁰ David added, "As the LORD lives, the LORD will certainly strike him down: either his day will come and he will die, or he will go into battle and perish. ¹¹ However, as the LORD is my witness, I will never lift my hand against the LORD's anointed. Instead, take the spear and the water jug by his head, and let's go."

¹² So David took the spear and the water jug by Saul's head, and they went their way. No one saw them, no one knew, and no one woke up; they all remained asleep because a deep sleep from the LORD came over them. ¹³ David crossed to the other side and stood on top of the mountain at a distance; there was a considerable space between them. ¹⁴ Then David shouted to the troops and to Abner son of Ner, "Aren't you going to answer, Abner?"

"Who are you who calls to the king?" Abner asked.

¹⁵ David called to Abner, "You're a man, aren't you? Who in Israel is your equal? So why didn't you protect your lord the king when one of the people came to destroy him? ¹⁶ What you have done is not good. As the LORD lives, all of you deserve to die since you didn't protect your lord, the LORD's anointed. Now look around; where are the king's spear and water jug that were by his head?"

¹⁷ Saul recognized David's voice and asked, "Is that your voice, my son David?"

"It is my voice, my lord and king," David said. ¹⁸ Then he continued, "Why is my lord pursuing his servant? What have I done? What crime have I committed? ¹⁹ Now, may my lord the king please hear the words of his servant: If it is the LORD who has incited you against me, then may he accept an offering. But if it is people, may they be cursed in the presence of the LORD,

for today they have banished me from sharing in the inheritance of the LORD, saying, 'Go and worship other gods.' ²⁰ So don't let my blood fall to the ground far from the LORD's presence, for the king of Israel has come out to search for a single flea, like one who pursues a partridge in the mountains."

²¹ Saul responded, "I have sinned. Come back, my son David, I will never harm you again because today you considered my life precious. I have been a fool! I've committed a grave error."

²² David answered, "Here is the king's spear; have one of the young men come over and get it. ²³ The LORD will repay every man for his righteousness and his loyalty. I wasn't willing to lift my hand against the LORD's anointed, even though the LORD handed you over to me today. ²⁴ Just as I considered your life valuable today, so may the LORD consider my life valuable and rescue me from all trouble."

²⁵ Saul said to him, "You are blessed, my son David. You will certainly do great things and will also prevail." Then David went on his way, and Saul returned home.

David Flees to Ziklag

27 David said to himself, "One of these days I'll be swept away by Saul. There is nothing better for me than to escape immediately to the land of the Philistines. Then Saul will give up searching for me everywhere in Israel, and I'll escape from him." ² So David set out with his six hundred men and went over to Achish son of Maoch, the king of Gath. ³ David and his men stayed with Achish in Gath. Each man had his family with him, and David had his two wives: Ahinoam of Jezreel and Abigail of Carmel, Nabal's widow. ⁴ When it was reported to Saul that David had fled to Gath, he no longer searched for him.

⁵ Now David said to Achish, "If I have found favor with you, let me be given a place in one of the outlying towns, so I can live there. Why should your servant live in the royal city with you?"

⁶ That day Achish gave Ziklag to him, and it still belongs to the kings of Judah today. ⁷ The length of time that David stayed in Philistine territory amounted to a year and four months.

⁸ David and his men went up and raided the Geshurites, the Girzites, and the Amalekites. From ancient times they had been the inhabitants of the region through Shur as far as the land of Egypt. ⁹ Whenever David attacked the land, he did not leave a single person alive, either man or woman, but he took flocks, herds, donkeys, camels, and clothing. Then he came back to Achish, ¹⁰ who inquired, "Where did you raid today?"

David replied, "The south country of Judah," "The south country of the Jerahmeelites," or "The south country of the Kenites."

¹¹ David did not let a man or woman live to be brought to Gath, for he said, "Or they will inform on us and say, 'This is what David did.'" This was David's custom during the whole time he stayed in the Philistine territory. ¹² So Achish trusted David, thinking, "Since he has made himself repulsive to his people Israel, he will be my servant forever."

Saul and the Medium

28 At that time, the Philistines gathered their military units into one army to fight against Israel. So Achish said to David, "You know, of course, that you and your men must march out in the army with me."

² David replied to Achish, "Good, you will find out what your servant can do."

So Achish said to David, "Very well, I will appoint you as my permanent bodyguard."

³ By this time Samuel had died, all Israel had mourned for him and buried him in Ramah, his city, and Saul had removed the mediums and spiritists from the land. ⁴ The Philistines gathered and camped at Shunem. So Saul gathered all Israel, and they camped at Gilboa. ⁵ When Saul saw the Philistine

camp, he was afraid and his heart pounded. [6] He inquired of the LORD, but the LORD did not answer him in dreams or by the Urim or by the prophets. [7] Saul then said to his servants, "Find me a woman who is a medium, so I can go and consult her."

His servants replied, "There is a woman at En-dor who is a medium."

[8] Saul disguised himself by putting on different clothes and set out with two of his men. They came to the woman at night, and Saul said, "Consult a spirit for me. Bring up for me the one I tell you."

[9] But the woman said to him, "You surely know what Saul has done, how he has cut off the mediums and spiritists from the land. Why are you setting a trap for me to get me killed?"

[10] Then Saul swore to her by the LORD: "As surely as the LORD lives, no punishment will come to you from this."

[11] "Who is it that you want me to bring up for you?" the woman asked.

"Bring up Samuel for me," he answered.

[12] When the woman saw Samuel, she screamed, and then she asked Saul, "Why did you deceive me? You are Saul!"

[13] But the king said to her, "Don't be afraid. What do you see?"

"I see a spirit form coming up out of the earth," the woman answered.

[14] Then Saul asked her, "What does he look like?"

"An old man is coming up," she replied. "He's wearing a robe." Then Saul knew that it was Samuel, and he knelt low with his face to the ground and paid homage.

[15] "Why have you disturbed me by bringing me up?" Samuel asked Saul.

"I'm in serious trouble," replied Saul. "The Philistines are fighting against me and God has turned away from me. He doesn't answer me anymore, either through the prophets or in dreams. So I've called on you to tell me what I should do."

¹⁶ Samuel answered, "Since the LORD has turned away from you and has become your enemy, why are you asking me? ¹⁷ The LORD has done exactly what he said through me: The LORD has torn the kingship out of your hand and given it to your neighbor David. ¹⁸ You did not obey the LORD and did not carry out his burning anger against Amalek; therefore the LORD has done this to you today. ¹⁹ The LORD will also hand Israel over to the Philistines along with you. Tomorrow you and your sons will be with me, and the LORD will hand Israel's army over to the Philistines."

²⁰ Immediately, Saul fell flat on the ground. He was terrified by Samuel's words and was also weak because he had not eaten anything all day and all night. ²¹ The woman came over to Saul, and she saw that he was terrified and said to him, "Look, your servant has obeyed you. I took my life in my hands and did what you told me to do. ²² Now please listen to your servant. Let me set some food in front of you. Eat and it will give you strength so you can go on your way."

²³ He refused, saying, "I won't eat," but when his servants and the woman urged him, he listened to them. He got up off the ground and sat on the bed.

²⁴ The woman had a fattened calf at her house, and she quickly slaughtered it. She also took flour, kneaded it, and baked unleavened bread. ²⁵ She served it to Saul and his servants, and they ate. Afterward, they got up and left that night.

Philistines Reject David

29 The Philistines brought all their military units together at Aphek while Israel was camped by the spring in Jezreel. ² As the Philistine leaders were passing in review with their units of hundreds and thousands, David and his men were passing in review behind them with Achish. ³ Then the Philistine commanders asked, "What are these Hebrews doing here?"

Achish answered the Philistine commanders, "That is David, servant of King Saul of Israel. He has been with me a considerable period of time. From the day he defected until today, I've found no fault with him."

⁴ The Philistine commanders, however, were enraged with Achish and told him, "Send that man back and let him return to the place you assigned him. He must not go down with us into battle only to become our adversary during the battle. What better way could he ingratiate himself with his master than with the heads of our men? ⁵ Isn't this the David they sing about during their dances:

Saul has killed his thousands,
but David his tens of thousands?"

⁶ So Achish summoned David and told him, "As the LORD lives, you are an honorable man. I think it is good to have you fighting in this unit with me, because I have found no fault in you from the day you came to me until today. But the leaders don't think you are reliable. ⁷ Now go back quietly and you won't be doing anything the Philistine leaders think is wrong."

⁸ "But what have I done?" David replied to Achish. "From the first day I entered your service until today, what have you found against your servant to keep me from going to fight against the enemies of my lord the king?"

⁹ Achish answered David, "I'm convinced that you are as reliable as an angel of God. But the Philistine commanders have said, 'He must not go into battle with us.' ¹⁰ So get up early in the morning, you and your masters' servants who came with you. When you've all gotten up early, go as soon as it's light." ¹¹ So David and his men got up early in the morning to return to the land of the Philistines. And the Philistines went up to Jezreel.

David's Defeat of the Amalekites

30 David and his men arrived in Ziklag on the third day. The Amalekites had raided the Negev and attacked and burned Ziklag. ² They also had kidnapped the women and everyone in it from youngest to oldest. They had killed no one but had carried them off as they went on their way.

³ When David and his men arrived at the town, they found it burned. Their wives, sons, and daughters had been kidnapped. ⁴ David and the troops with him wept loudly until they had no strength left to weep. ⁵ David's two wives, Ahinoam the Jezreelite and Abigail the widow of Nabal the Carmelite, had also been kidnapped. ⁶ David was in an extremely difficult position because the troops talked about stoning him, for they were all very bitter over the loss of their sons and daughters. But David found strength in the LORD his God.

⁷ David said to the priest Abiathar son of Ahimelech, "Bring me the ephod." So Abiathar brought it to him, ⁸ and David asked the LORD, "Should I pursue these raiders? Will I overtake them?"

The LORD replied to him, "Pursue them, for you will certainly overtake them and rescue the people."

⁹ So David and the six hundred men with him went. They came to the Wadi Besor, where some stayed behind. ¹⁰ David and four hundred of the men continued the pursuit, while two hundred stopped because they were too exhausted to cross the Wadi Besor.

¹¹ David's men found an Egyptian in the open country and brought him to David. They gave him some bread to eat and water to drink. ¹² Then they gave him some pressed figs and two clusters of raisins. After he ate he revived, for he hadn't eaten food or drunk water for three days and three nights.

¹³ Then David said to him, "Who do you belong to? Where are you from?"

"I'm an Egyptian, the slave of an Amalekite man," he said. "My master abandoned me when I got sick three days ago. ¹⁴ We

raided the south country of the Cherethites, the territory of Judah, and the south country of Caleb, and we burned Ziklag."

15 David then asked him, "Will you lead me to these raiders?"

He said, "Swear to me by God that you won't kill me or turn me over to my master, and I will lead you to them."

16 So he led him, and there were the Amalekites, spread out over the entire area, eating, drinking, and celebrating because of the great amount of plunder they had taken from the land of the Philistines and the land of Judah. **17** David slaughtered them from twilight until the evening of the next day. None of them escaped, except four hundred young men who got on camels and fled.

18 David recovered everything the Amalekites had taken; he also rescued his two wives. **19** Nothing of theirs was missing from the youngest to the oldest, including the sons and daughters, and all the plunder the Amalekites had taken. David got everything back. **20** He took all the flocks and herds, which were driven ahead of the other livestock, and the people shouted, "This is David's plunder!"

21 When David came to the two hundred men who had been too exhausted to go with him and had been left at the Wadi Besor, they came out to meet him and to meet the troops with him. When David approached the men, he greeted them, **22** but all the corrupt and worthless men among those who had gone with David argued, "Because they didn't go with us, we will not give any of the plunder we recovered to them except for each man's wife and children. They may take them and go."

23 But David said, "My brothers, you must not do this with what the LORD has given us. He protected us and handed over to us the raiders who came against us. **24** Who can agree to your proposal? The share of the one who goes into battle is to be the same as the share of the one who remains with the supplies. They will share equally." **25** And it has been so from that

day forward. David established this policy as a law and an ordinance for Israel and it still continues today.

²⁶ When David came to Ziklag, he sent some of the plunder to his friends, the elders of Judah, saying, "Here is a gift for you from the plunder of the LORD's enemies." ²⁷ He sent gifts to those in Bethel, in Ramoth of the Negev, and in Jattir; ²⁸ to those in Aroer, in Siphmoth, and in Eshtemoa; ²⁹ to those in Racal, in the towns of the Jerahmeelites, and in the towns of the Kenites; ³⁰ to those in Hormah, in Bor-ashan, and in Athach; ³¹ to those in Hebron, and to those in all the places where David and his men had roamed.

The Death of Saul and His Sons

31 The Philistines fought against Israel, and Israel's men fled from them and were killed on Mount Gilboa. ² The Philistines pursued Saul and his sons and killed his sons, Jonathan, Abinadab, and Malchishua. ³ When the battle intensified against Saul, the archers found him and severely wounded him. ⁴ Then Saul said to his armor-bearer, "Draw your sword and run me through with it, or these uncircumcised men will come and run me through and torture me!" But his armor-bearer would not do it because he was terrified. Then Saul took his sword and fell on it. ⁵ When his armor-bearer saw that Saul was dead, he also fell on his own sword and died with him. ⁶ So on that day, Saul died together with his three sons, his armor-bearer, and all his men.

⁷ When the men of Israel on the other side of the valley and on the other side of the Jordan saw that Israel's men had fled and that Saul and his sons were dead, they abandoned the cities and fled. So the Philistines came and settled in them.

⁸ The next day when the Philistines came to strip the slain, they found Saul and his three sons dead on Mount Gilboa. ⁹ They cut off Saul's head, stripped off his armor, and sent

messengers throughout the land of the Philistines to spread the good news in the temples of their idols and among the people. ¹⁰ Then they put his armor in the temple of the Ashtoreths and hung his body on the wall of Beth-shan.

¹¹ When the residents of Jabesh-gilead heard what the Philistines had done to Saul, ¹² all their brave men set out, journeyed all night, and retrieved the body of Saul and the bodies of his sons from the wall of Beth-shan. When they arrived at Jabesh, they burned the bodies there. ¹³ Afterward, they took their bones and buried them under the tamarisk tree in Jabesh and fasted seven days.

2 SAMUEL

Responses to Saul's Death

1 After the death of Saul, David returned from defeating the Amalekites and stayed at Ziklag two days. ² On the third day a man with torn clothes and dust on his head came from Saul's camp. When he came to David, he fell to the ground and paid homage. ³ David asked him, "Where have you come from?"

He replied to him, "I've escaped from the Israelite camp."

⁴ "What was the outcome? Tell me," David asked him.

"The troops fled from the battle," he answered. "Many of the troops have fallen and are dead. Also, Saul and his son Jonathan are dead."

⁵ David asked the young man who had brought him the report, "How do you know Saul and his son Jonathan are dead?"

⁶ "I happened to be on Mount Gilboa," he replied, "and there was Saul, leaning on his spear. At that very moment the chariots and the cavalry were closing in on him. ⁷ When he turned around and saw me, he called out to me, so I answered: I'm at your service. ⁸ He asked me, 'Who are you?' I told him: I'm an Amalekite. ⁹ Then he begged me, 'Stand over me and kill me, for I'm mortally wounded, but my life still lingers.' ¹⁰ So I stood over him and killed him because I knew that after he had fallen he couldn't survive. I took the crown that was on his head and the armband that was on his arm, and I've brought them here to my lord."

¹¹ Then David took hold of his clothes and tore them, and all the men with him did the same. ¹² They mourned, wept, and fasted until the evening for those who died by the sword — for Saul, his son Jonathan, the LORD's people, and the house of Israel.

¹³ David inquired of the young man who had brought him the report, "Where are you from?"

"I'm the son of a resident alien," he said. "I'm an Amalekite."

¹⁴ David questioned him, "How is it that you were not afraid to lift your hand to destroy the LORD's anointed?" ¹⁵ Then David

summoned one of his servants and said, "Come here and kill him!" The servant struck him, and he died. ¹⁶ For David had said to the Amalekite, "Your blood is on your own head because your own mouth testified against you by saying, 'I killed the LORD's anointed.'"

¹⁷ David sang the following lament for Saul and his son Jonathan, ¹⁸ and he ordered that the Judahites be taught The Song of the Bow. It is written in the Book of Jashar:

¹⁹   The splendor of Israel lies slain on your heights.
     How the mighty have fallen!

²⁰   Do not tell it in Gath,
     don't announce it in the marketplaces of Ashkelon,
     or the daughters of the Philistines will rejoice,
     and the daughters of the uncircumcised will celebrate.

²¹   Mountains of Gilboa,
     let no dew or rain be on you,
     or fields of offerings,
     for there the shield of the mighty was defiled —
     the shield of Saul, no longer anointed with oil.

²²   Jonathan's bow never retreated,
     Saul's sword never returned unstained,
     from the blood of the slain,
     from the flesh of the mighty.

²³   Saul and Jonathan,
     loved and delightful,
     they were not parted in life or in death.
     They were swifter than eagles, stronger than lions.

²⁴   Daughters of Israel, weep for Saul,
     who clothed you in scarlet, with luxurious things,
     who decked your garments with gold ornaments.

²⁵   How the mighty have fallen in the thick of battle!
     Jonathan lies slain on your heights.

²⁶   I grieve for you, Jonathan, my brother.

You were such a friend to me.
Your love for me was more wondrous
than the love of women.
²⁷ How the mighty have fallen
and the weapons of war have perished!

David, King of Judah

2 Some time later, David inquired of the LORD: "Should I go to one of the towns of Judah?"

The LORD answered him, "Go."

Then David asked, "Where should I go?"

"To Hebron," the LORD replied.

² So David went there with his two wives, Ahinoam the Jezreelite and Abigail, the widow of Nabal the Carmelite. ³ In addition, David brought the men who were with him, each one with his family, and they settled in the towns near Hebron. ⁴ Then the men of Judah came, and there they anointed David king over the house of Judah. They told David, "It was the men of Jabesh-gilead who buried Saul."

⁵ David sent messengers to the men of Jabesh-gilead and said to them, "The LORD bless you because you have shown this kindness to Saul your lord when you buried him. ⁶ Now, may the LORD show kindness and faithfulness to you, and I will also show the same goodness to you because you have done this deed. ⁷ Therefore, be strong and valiant, for though Saul your lord is dead, the house of Judah has anointed me king over them."

⁸ Abner son of Ner, commander of Saul's army, took Saul's son Ish-bosheth and moved him to Mahanaim. ⁹ He made him king over Gilead, Asher, Jezreel, Ephraim, Benjamin — over all Israel. ¹⁰ Saul's son Ish-bosheth was forty years old when he became king over Israel; he reigned for two years. The house of Judah, however, followed David. ¹¹ The length of time that David

was king in Hebron over the house of Judah was seven years and six months.

¹² Abner son of Ner and soldiers of Ish-bosheth son of Saul marched out from Mahanaim to Gibeon. ¹³ So Joab son of Zeruiah and David's soldiers marched out and met them by the pool of Gibeon. The two groups took up positions on opposite sides of the pool.

¹⁴ Then Abner said to Joab, "Let's have the young men get up and compete in front of us."

"Let them get up," Joab replied.

¹⁵ So they got up and were counted off — twelve for Benjamin and Ish-bosheth son of Saul, and twelve from David's soldiers. ¹⁶ Then each man grabbed his opponent by the head and thrust his sword into his opponent's side so that they all died together. So this place, which is in Gibeon, is named Field of Blades.

¹⁷ The battle that day was extremely fierce, and Abner and the men of Israel were defeated by David's soldiers. ¹⁸ The three sons of Zeruiah were there: Joab, Abishai, and Asahel. Asahel was a fast runner, like one of the wild gazelles. ¹⁹ He chased Abner and did not turn to the right or the left in his pursuit of him. ²⁰ Abner glanced back and said, "Is that you, Asahel?"

"Yes it is," Asahel replied.

²¹ Abner said to him, "Turn to your right or left, seize one of the young soldiers, and take whatever you can get from him." But Asahel would not stop chasing him. ²² Once again, Abner warned Asahel, "Stop chasing me. Why should I strike you to the ground? How could I ever look your brother Joab in the face?"

²³ But Asahel refused to turn away, so Abner hit him in the stomach with the butt of his spear. The spear went through his body, and he fell and died right there. As they all came to the place where Asahel had fallen and died, they stopped, ²⁴ but

Joab and Abishai pursued Abner. By sunset, they had gone as far as the hill of Ammah, which is opposite Giah on the way to the wilderness of Gibeon.

²⁵ The Benjaminites rallied to Abner; they formed a unit and took their stand on top of a hill. ²⁶ Then Abner called out to Joab, "Must the sword devour forever? Don't you realize this will only end in bitterness? How long before you tell the troops to stop pursuing their brothers? "

²⁷ "As God lives," Joab replied, "if you had not spoken up, the troops wouldn't have stopped pursuing their brothers until morning." ²⁸ Then Joab blew the ram's horn, and all the troops stopped; they no longer pursued Israel or continued to fight. ²⁹ So Abner and his men marched through the Arabah all that night. They crossed the Jordan, marched all morning, and arrived at Mahanaim.

³⁰ When Joab had turned back from pursuing Abner, he gathered all the troops. In addition to Asahel, nineteen of David's soldiers were missing, ³¹ but they had killed 360 of the Benjaminites and Abner's men. ³² Afterward, they carried Asahel to his father's tomb in Bethlehem and buried him. Then Joab and his men marched all night and reached Hebron at dawn.

Civil War

3 During the long war between the house of Saul and the house of David, David was growing stronger and the house of Saul was becoming weaker.

² Sons were born to David in Hebron:
His firstborn was Amnon,
by Ahinoam the Jezreelite;
³ his second was Chileab,
by Abigail, the widow of Nabal the Carmelite;
the third was Absalom,
son of Maacah the daughter of King Talmai of Geshur;

⁴ the fourth was Adonijah,
son of Haggith;
the fifth was Shephatiah,
son of Abital;
⁵ the sixth was Ithream,
by David's wife Eglah.
These were born to David in Hebron.

⁶ During the war between the house of Saul and the house of David, Abner kept acquiring more power in the house of Saul. ⁷ Now Saul had a concubine whose name was Rizpah daughter of Aiah, and Ish-bosheth questioned Abner, "Why did you sleep with my father's concubine?"

⁸ Abner was very angry about Ish-bosheth's accusation. "Am I a dog's head who belongs to Judah?" he asked. "All this time I've been loyal to the family of your father Saul, to his brothers, and to his friends and haven't betrayed you to David, but now you accuse me of wrongdoing with this woman! ⁹ May God punish Abner and do so severely if I don't do for David what the LORD swore to him: ¹⁰ to transfer the kingdom from the house of Saul and establish the throne of David over Israel and Judah from Dan to Beer-sheba." ¹¹ Ish-bosheth did not dare respond to Abner because he was afraid of him.

¹² Abner sent messengers as his representatives to say to David, "Whose land is it? Make your covenant with me, and you can be certain I am on your side to turn all Israel over to you."

¹³ David replied, "Good, I will make a covenant with you. However, there's one thing I require of you: You will not see my face unless you first bring Saul's daughter Michal when you come to see me."

¹⁴ Then David sent messengers to say to Ish-bosheth son of Saul, "Give me back my wife Michal. I was engaged to her for the price of a hundred Philistine foreskins."

¹⁵ So Ish-bosheth sent someone to take her away from her husband, Paltiel son of Laish. ¹⁶ Her husband followed her, weeping all the way to Bahurim. Abner said to him, "Go back." So he went back.

The Assassination of Abner

¹⁷ Abner conferred with the elders of Israel: "In the past you wanted David to be king over you. ¹⁸ Now take action, because the LORD has spoken concerning David: 'Through my servant David I will save my people Israel from the power of the Philistines and the power of all Israel's enemies.'"

¹⁹ Abner also informed the Benjaminites and went to Hebron to inform David about all that was agreed on by Israel and the whole house of Benjamin. ²⁰ When Abner and twenty men came to David at Hebron, David held a banquet for him and his men.

²¹ Abner said to David, "Let me now go and I will gather all Israel to my lord the king. They will make a covenant with you, and you will reign over all you desire." So David dismissed Abner, and he went in peace.

²² Just then David's soldiers and Joab returned from a raid and brought a large amount of plundered goods with them. Abner was not with David in Hebron because David had dismissed him, and he had gone in peace. ²³ When Joab and his whole army arrived, Joab was informed, "Abner son of Ner came to see the king, the king dismissed him, and he went in peace."

²⁴ Joab went to the king and said, "What have you done? Look here, Abner came to you. Why did you dismiss him? Now he's getting away. ²⁵ You know that Abner son of Ner came to deceive you and to find out about your military activities and everything you're doing." ²⁶ Then Joab left David and sent messengers after Abner. They brought him back from the well of

Sirah, but David was unaware of it. ²⁷ When Abner returned to Hebron, Joab pulled him aside to the middle of the city gate, as if to speak to him privately, and there Joab stabbed him in the stomach. So Abner died in revenge for the death of Asahel, Joab's brother.

²⁸ David heard about it later and said, "I and my kingdom are forever innocent before the LORD concerning the blood of Abner son of Ner. ²⁹ May it hang over Joab's head and his father's whole family, and may the house of Joab never be without someone who has a discharge or a skin disease, or a man who can only work a spindle, or someone who falls by the sword or starves." ³⁰ Joab and his brother Abishai killed Abner because he had put their brother Asahel to death in the battle at Gibeon.

³¹ David then ordered Joab and all the people who were with him, "Tear your clothes, put on sackcloth, and mourn over Abner." And King David walked behind the coffin.

³² When they buried Abner in Hebron, the king wept aloud at Abner's tomb. All the people wept, ³³ and the king sang a lament for Abner:

Should Abner die as a fool dies?
³⁴   Your hands were not bound,
your feet not placed in bronze shackles.
You fell like one who falls victim to criminals.
And all the people wept over him even more.

³⁵ Then they came to urge David to eat food while it was still day, but David took an oath: "May God punish me and do so severely if I taste bread or anything else before sunset!" ³⁶ All the people took note of this, and it pleased them. In fact, everything the king did pleased them. ³⁷ On that day all the troops and all Israel were convinced that the king had no part in the killing of Abner son of Ner.

³⁸ Then the king said to his soldiers, "You must know that a great leader has fallen in Israel today. ³⁹ As for me, even though

I am the anointed king, I have little power today. These men, the sons of Zeruiah, are too fierce for me. May the LORD repay the evildoer according to his evil! "

The Assassination of Ish-bosheth

4 When Saul's son Ish-bosheth heard that Abner had died in Hebron, he gave up, and all Israel was dismayed. ² Saul's son had two men who were leaders of raiding parties: one named Baanah and the other Rechab, sons of Rimmon the Beerothite of the Benjaminites. Beeroth is also considered part of Benjamin, ³ and the Beerothites fled to Gittaim and still reside there as aliens today.

⁴ Saul's son Jonathan had a son whose feet were crippled. He was five years old when the report about Saul and Jonathan came from Jezreel. His nanny picked him up and fled, but as she was hurrying to flee, he fell and became lame. His name was Mephibosheth.

⁵ Rechab and Baanah, the sons of Rimmon the Beerothite, set out and arrived at Ish-bosheth's house during the heat of the day while the king was taking his midday nap. ⁶ They entered the interior of the house as if to get wheat and stabbed him in the stomach. Then Rechab and his brother Baanah escaped. ⁷ They had entered the house while Ish-bosheth was lying on his bed in his bedroom and stabbed and killed him. They removed his head, took it, and traveled by way of the Arabah all night. ⁸ They brought Ish-bosheth's head to David at Hebron and said to the king, "Here's the head of Ish-bosheth son of Saul, your enemy who intended to take your life. Today the LORD has granted vengeance to my lord the king against Saul and his offspring."

⁹ But David answered Rechab and his brother Baanah, sons of Rimmon the Beerothite, "As the LORD lives, the one who has redeemed my life from every distress, ¹⁰ when the person told

me, 'Look, Saul is dead,' he thought he was a bearer of good news, but I seized him and put him to death at Ziklag. That was my reward to him for his news! ¹¹ How much more when wicked men kill a righteous man in his own house on his own bed! So now, should I not require his blood from you and purge you from the earth?"

¹² So David gave orders to the young men, and they killed Rechab and Baanah. They cut off their hands and feet and hung their bodies by the pool in Hebron, but they took Ish-bosheth's head and buried it in Abner's tomb in Hebron.

David, King of Israel

5 All the tribes of Israel came to David at Hebron and said, "Here we are, your own flesh and blood. ² Even while Saul was king over us, you were the one who led us out to battle and brought us back. The Lord also said to you, 'You will shepherd my people Israel, and you will be ruler over Israel.'"

³ So all the elders of Israel came to the king at Hebron. King David made a covenant with them at Hebron in the Lord's presence, and they anointed David king over Israel.

⁴ David was thirty years old when he began his reign; he reigned forty years. ⁵ In Hebron he reigned over Judah seven years and six months, and in Jerusalem he reigned thirty-three years over all Israel and Judah.

⁶ The king and his men marched to Jerusalem against the Jebusites who inhabited the land. The Jebusites had said to David, "You will never get in here. Even the blind and lame can repel you" thinking, "David can't get in here."

⁷ Yet David did capture the stronghold of Zion, that is, the city of David. ⁸ He said that day, "Whoever attacks the Jebusites must go through the water shaft to reach the lame and the blind who are despised by David." For this reason it is said, "The blind and the lame will never enter the house."

⁹ David took up residence in the stronghold, which he named the city of David. He built it up all the way around from the supporting terraces inward. ¹⁰ David became more and more powerful, and the LORD God of Armies was with him. ¹¹ King Hiram of Tyre sent envoys to David; he also sent cedar logs, carpenters, and stonemasons, and they built a palace for David. ¹² Then David knew that the LORD had established him as king over Israel and had exalted his kingdom for the sake of his people Israel.

¹³ After he arrived from Hebron, David took more concubines and wives from Jerusalem, and more sons and daughters were born to him. ¹⁴ These are the names of those born to him in Jerusalem: Shammua, Shobab, Nathan, Solomon, ¹⁵ Ibhar, Elishua, Nepheg, Japhia, ¹⁶ Elishama, Eliada, and Eliphelet.

¹⁷ When the Philistines heard that David had been anointed king over Israel, they all went in search of David, but he heard about it and went down to the stronghold. ¹⁸ So the Philistines came and spread out in Rephaim Valley.

¹⁹ Then David inquired of the LORD: "Should I attack the Philistines? Will you hand them over to me?"

The LORD replied to David, "Attack, for I will certainly hand the Philistines over to you."

²⁰ So David went to Baal-perazim and defeated them there and said, "Like a bursting flood, the LORD has burst out against my enemies before me." Therefore, he named that place The Lord Bursts Out. ²¹ The Philistines abandoned their idols there, and David and his men carried them off.

²² The Philistines came up again and spread out in Rephaim Valley. ²³ So David inquired of the LORD, and he answered, "Do not attack directly, but circle around behind them and come at them opposite the balsam trees. ²⁴ When you hear the sound of marching in the tops of the balsam trees, act decisively, for then the LORD will have gone out ahead of you to strike down the army of the Philistines." ²⁵ So David did exactly as the LORD

commanded him, and he struck down the Philistines all the way from Geba to Gezer.

David Moves the Ark

6 David again assembled all the fit young men in Israel: thirty thousand. ² He and all his troops set out to bring the ark of God from Baale-judah. The ark bears the Name, the name of the LORD of Armies who is enthroned between the cherubim. ³ They set the ark of God on a new cart and transported it from Abinadab's house, which was on the hill. Uzzah and Ahio, sons of Abinadab, were guiding the cart ⁴ and brought it with the ark of God from Abinadab's house on the hill. Ahio walked in front of the ark. ⁵ David and the whole house of Israel were dancing before the LORD with all kinds of fir wood instruments, lyres, harps, tambourines, sistrums, and cymbals.

⁶ When they came to Nacon's threshing floor, Uzzah reached out to the ark of God and took hold of it because the oxen had stumbled. ⁷ Then the LORD's anger burned against Uzzah, and God struck him dead on the spot for his irreverence, and he died there next to the ark of God. ⁸ David was angry because of the LORD's outburst against Uzzah, so he named that place Outburst Against Uzzah, as it is today. ⁹ David feared the LORD that day and said, "How can the ark of the LORD ever come to me?" ¹⁰ So he was not willing to bring the ark of the LORD to the city of David; instead, he diverted it to the house of Obed-edom of Gath. ¹¹ The ark of the LORD remained in his house three months, and the LORD blessed Obed-edom and his whole family.

¹² It was reported to King David, "The LORD has blessed Obed-edom's family and all that belongs to him because of the ark of God." So David went and had the ark of God brought up from Obed-edom's house to the city of David with rejoicing. ¹³ When those carrying the ark of the LORD advanced six steps,

he sacrificed an ox and a fattened calf. ¹⁴ David was dancing with all his might before the LORD wearing a linen ephod. ¹⁵ He and the whole house of Israel were bringing up the ark of the LORD with shouts and the sound of the ram's horn. ¹⁶ As the ark of the LORD was entering the city of David, Saul's daughter Michal looked down from the window and saw King David leaping and dancing before the LORD, and she despised him in her heart.

¹⁷ They brought the ark of the LORD and set it in its place inside the tent David had pitched for it. Then David offered burnt offerings and fellowship offerings in the LORD's presence. ¹⁸ When David had finished offering the burnt offering and the fellowship offerings, he blessed the people in the name of the LORD of Armies. ¹⁹ Then he distributed a loaf of bread, a date cake, and a raisin cake to each one in the entire Israelite community, both men and women. Then all the people went home.

²⁰ When David returned home to bless his household, Saul's daughter Michal came out to meet him. "How the king of Israel honored himself today!" she said. "He exposed himself today in the sight of the slave girls of his subjects like a vulgar person would expose himself."

²¹ David replied to Michal, "It was before the LORD who chose me over your father and his whole family to appoint me ruler over the LORD's people Israel. I will dance before the LORD, ²² and I will dishonor myself and humble myself even more. However, by the slave girls you spoke about, I will be honored." ²³ And Saul's daughter Michal had no child to the day of her death.

The LORD's Covenant with David

7 When the king had settled into his palace and the LORD had given him rest on every side from all his enemies, ² the king said to the prophet Nathan, "Look, I am living in a cedar house while the ark of God sits inside tent curtains."

³ So Nathan told the king, "Go and do all that is on your mind, for the LORD is with you."

⁴ But that night the word of the LORD came to Nathan: ⁵ "Go to my servant David and say, 'This is what the LORD says: Are you to build me a house to dwell in? ⁶ From the time I brought the Israelites out of Egypt until today I have not dwelt in a house; instead, I have been moving around with a tent as my dwelling. ⁷ In all my journeys with all the Israelites, have I ever spoken a word to one of the tribal leaders of Israel, whom I commanded to shepherd my people Israel, asking: Why haven't you built me a house of cedar?'

⁸ "So now this is what you are to say to my servant David: 'This is what the LORD of Armies says: I took you from the pasture, from tending the flock, to be ruler over my people Israel. ⁹ I have been with you wherever you have gone, and I have destroyed all your enemies before you. I will make a great name for you like that of the greatest on the earth. ¹⁰ I will designate a place for my people Israel and plant them, so that they may live there and not be disturbed again. Evildoers will not continue to oppress them as they have done ¹¹ ever since the day I ordered judges to be over my people Israel. I will give you rest from all your enemies.

"'The LORD declares to you: The LORD himself will make a house for you. ¹² When your time comes and you rest with your ancestors, I will raise up after you your descendant, who will come from your body, and I will establish his kingdom. ¹³ He is the one who will build a house for my name, and I will establish the throne of his kingdom forever. ¹⁴ I will be his father, and he will be my son. When he does wrong, I will discipline him with a rod of men and blows from mortals. ¹⁵ But my faithful love will never leave him as it did when I removed it from Saul, whom I removed from before you. ¹⁶ Your house and kingdom will endure before me forever, and your throne will be established forever.'"

¹⁷ Nathan reported all these words and this entire vision to David.

David's Prayer of Thanksgiving

¹⁸ Then King David went in, sat in the LORD's presence, and said, Who am I, Lord GOD, and what is my house that you have brought me this far? ¹⁹ What you have done so far was a little thing to you, Lord GOD, for you have also spoken about your servant's house in the distant future. And this is a revelation for mankind, Lord GOD. ²⁰ What more can David say to you? You know your servant, Lord GOD. ²¹ Because of your word and according to your will, you have revealed all these great things to your servant.

²² This is why you are great, Lord GOD. There is no one like you, and there is no God besides you, as all we have heard confirms. ²³ And who is like your people Israel? God came to one nation on earth in order to redeem a people for himself, to make a name for himself, and to perform for them great and awesome acts, driving out nations and their gods before your people you redeemed for yourself from Egypt. ²⁴ You established your people Israel to be your own people forever, and you, LORD, have become their God.

²⁵ Now, LORD God, fulfill the promise forever that you have made to your servant and his house. Do as you have promised, ²⁶ so that your name will be exalted forever, when it is said, "The LORD of Armies is God over Israel." The house of your servant David will be established before you ²⁷ since you, LORD of Armies, God of Israel, have revealed this to your servant when you said, "I will build a house for you." Therefore, your servant has found the courage to pray this prayer to you. ²⁸ Lord GOD, you are God; your words are true, and you

have promised this good thing to your servant. ²⁹ Now, please bless your servant's house so that it will continue before you forever. For you, Lord GOD, have spoken, and with your blessing your servant's house will be blessed forever.

David's Victories

8 After this, David defeated the Philistines, subdued them, and took Metheg-ammah from Philistine control. ² He also defeated the Moabites, and after making them lie down on the ground, he measured them off with a cord. He measured every two cord lengths of those to be put to death and one full length of those to be kept alive. So the Moabites became David's subjects and brought tribute.

³ David also defeated Hadadezer son of Rehob, king of Zobah, when he went to restore his control at the Euphrates River. ⁴ David captured seventeen hundred horsemen and twenty thousand foot soldiers from him, and he hamstrung all the horses and kept a hundred chariots.

⁵ When the Arameans of Damascus came to assist King Hadadezer of Zobah, David struck down twenty-two thousand Aramean men. ⁶ Then he placed garrisons in Aram of Damascus, and the Arameans became David's subjects and brought tribute. The LORD made David victorious wherever he went.

⁷ David took the gold shields of Hadadezer's officers and brought them to Jerusalem. ⁸ King David also took huge quantities of bronze from Betah and Berothai, Hadadezer's cities.

⁹ When King Toi of Hamath heard that David had defeated the entire army of Hadadezer, ¹⁰ he sent his son Joram to King David to greet him and to congratulate him because David had fought against Hadadezer and defeated him, for Toi and Hadadezer had fought many wars. Joram had items of silver, gold, and bronze with him. ¹¹ King David also dedicated these to the LORD, along with the silver and gold he had dedicated from all

the nations he had subdued — ¹² from Edom, Moab, the Ammonites, the Philistines, the Amalekites, and the spoil of Hadadezer son of Rehob, king of Zobah.

¹³ David made a reputation for himself when he returned from striking down eighteen thousand Edomites in Salt Valley. ¹⁴ He placed garrisons throughout Edom, and all the Edomites were subject to David. The LORD made David victorious wherever he went.

¹⁵ So David reigned over all Israel, administering justice and righteousness for all his people.

¹⁶   Joab son of Zeruiah was over the army;
    Jehoshaphat son of Ahilud was court historian;
¹⁷   Zadok son of Ahitub and Ahimelech son of Abiathar
        were priests;
    Seraiah was court secretary;
¹⁸   Benaiah son of Jehoiada was over the Cherethites
        and the Pelethites;
    and David's sons were chief officials.

David's Kindness to Mephibosheth

9 David asked, "Is there anyone remaining from the family of Saul I can show kindness to for Jonathan's sake?" ² There was a servant of Saul's family named Ziba. They summoned him to David, and the king said to him, "Are you Ziba?"

"I am your servant," he replied.

³ So the king asked, "Is there anyone left of Saul's family that I can show the kindness of God to?"

Ziba said to the king, "There is still Jonathan's son who was injured in both feet."

⁴ The king asked him, "Where is he?"

Ziba answered the king, "You'll find him in Lo-debar at the house of Machir son of Ammiel." ⁵ So King David had him brought from the house of Machir son of Ammiel in Lo-debar.

⁶ Mephibosheth son of Jonathan son of Saul came to David, fell facedown, and paid homage. David said, "Mephibosheth!"

"I am your servant," he replied.

⁷ "Don't be afraid," David said to him, "since I intend to show you kindness for the sake of your father Jonathan. I will restore to you all your grandfather Saul's fields, and you will always eat meals at my table."

⁸ Mephibosheth paid homage and said, "What is your servant that you take an interest in a dead dog like me?"

⁹ Then the king summoned Saul's attendant Ziba and said to him, "I have given to your master's grandson all that belonged to Saul and his family. ¹⁰ You, your sons, and your servants are to work the ground for him, and you are to bring in the crops so your master's grandson will have food to eat. But Mephibosheth, your master's grandson, is always to eat at my table." Now Ziba had fifteen sons and twenty servants.

¹¹ Ziba said to the king, "Your servant will do all my lord the king commands."

So Mephibosheth ate at David's table just like one of the king's sons. ¹² Mephibosheth had a young son whose name was Mica. All those living in Ziba's house were Mephibosheth's servants. ¹³ However, Mephibosheth lived in Jerusalem because he always ate at the king's table. His feet had been injured.

War with the Ammonites

10 Some time later, the king of the Ammonites died, and his son Hanun became king in his place. ² Then David said, "I'll show kindness to Hanun son of Nahash, just as his father showed kindness to me."

So David sent his emissaries to console Hanun concerning his father. However, when they arrived in the land of the Ammonites, ³ the Ammonite leaders said to Hanun their lord, "Just because David has sent men with condolences for you, do you

really believe he's showing respect for your father? Instead, hasn't David sent his emissaries in order to scout out the city, spy on it, and demolish it?" ⁴ So Hanun took David's emissaries, shaved off half their beards, cut their clothes in half at the hips, and sent them away.

⁵ When this was reported to David, he sent someone to meet them, since they were deeply humiliated. The king said, "Stay in Jericho until your beards grow back; then return."

⁶ When the Ammonites realized they had become repulsive to David, they hired twenty thousand foot soldiers from the Arameans of Beth-rehob and Zobah, one thousand men from the king of Maacah, and twelve thousand men from Tob.

⁷ David heard about it and sent Joab and all the elite troops. ⁸ The Ammonites marched out and lined up in battle formation at the entrance to the city gate while the Arameans of Zobah and Rehob and the men of Tob and Maacah were in the field by themselves. ⁹ When Joab saw that there was a battle line in front of him and another behind him, he chose some of Israel's finest young men and lined up in formation to engage the Arameans. ¹⁰ He placed the rest of the forces under the command of his brother Abishai. They lined up in formation to engage the Ammonites.

¹¹ "If the Arameans are too strong for me," Joab said, "then you will be my help. However, if the Ammonites are too strong for you, I'll come to help you. ¹² Be strong! Let's prove ourselves strong for our people and for the cities of our God. May the LORD's will be done."

¹³ Joab and his troops advanced to fight against the Arameans, and they fled before him. ¹⁴ When the Ammonites saw that the Arameans had fled, they too fled before Abishai and entered the city. So Joab withdrew from the attack against the Ammonites and went to Jerusalem.

¹⁵ When the Arameans saw that they had been defeated by Israel, they regrouped. ¹⁶ Hadadezer sent messengers to bring

the Arameans who were beyond the Euphrates River, and they came to Helam with Shobach, commander of Hadadezer's army, leading them.

¹⁷ When this was reported to David, he gathered all Israel, crossed the Jordan, and went to Helam. Then the Arameans lined up to engage David in battle and fought against him. ¹⁸ But the Arameans fled before Israel, and David killed seven hundred of their charioteers and forty thousand foot soldiers. He also struck down Shobach commander of their army, who died there. ¹⁹ When all the kings who were Hadadezer's subjects saw that they had been defeated by Israel, they made peace with Israel and became their subjects. After this, the Arameans were afraid to ever help the Ammonites again.

David's Adultery with Bathsheba

11 In the spring when kings march out to war, David sent Joab with his officers and all Israel. They destroyed the Ammonites and besieged Rabbah, but David remained in Jerusalem.

² One evening David got up from his bed and strolled around on the roof of the palace. From the roof he saw a woman bathing — a very beautiful woman. ³ So David sent someone to inquire about her, and he said, "Isn't this Bathsheba, daughter of Eliam and wife of Uriah the Hethite?"

⁴ David sent messengers to get her, and when she came to him, he slept with her. Now she had just been purifying herself from her uncleanness. Afterward, she returned home. ⁵ The woman conceived and sent word to inform David, "I am pregnant."

⁶ David sent orders to Joab: "Send me Uriah the Hethite." So Joab sent Uriah to David. ⁷ When Uriah came to him, David asked how Joab and the troops were doing and how the war was going. ⁸ Then he said to Uriah, "Go down to your house and

wash your feet." So Uriah left the palace, and a gift from the king followed him. ⁹ But Uriah slept at the door of the palace with all his master's servants; he did not go down to his house.

¹⁰ When it was reported to David, "Uriah didn't go home," David questioned Uriah, "Haven't you just come from a journey? Why didn't you go home?"

¹¹ Uriah answered David, "The ark, Israel, and Judah are dwelling in tents, and my master Joab and his soldiers are camping in the open field. How can I enter my house to eat and drink and sleep with my wife? As surely as you live and by your life, I will not do this!"

¹² "Stay here today also," David said to Uriah, "and tomorrow I will send you back." So Uriah stayed in Jerusalem that day and the next. ¹³ Then David invited Uriah to eat and drink with him, and David got him drunk. He went out in the evening to lie down on his cot with his master's servants, but he did not go home.

Uriah's Death Arranged

¹⁴ The next morning David wrote a letter to Joab and sent it with Uriah. ¹⁵ In the letter he wrote:

Put Uriah at the front of the fiercest fighting, then withdraw from him so that he is struck down and dies.

¹⁶ When Joab was besieging the city, he put Uriah in the place where he knew the best enemy soldiers were. ¹⁷ Then the men of the city came out and attacked Joab, and some of the men from David's soldiers fell in battle; Uriah the Hethite also died.

¹⁸ Joab sent someone to report to David all the details of the battle. ¹⁹ He commanded the messenger, "When you've finished telling the king all the details of the battle — ²⁰ if the king's anger gets stirred up and he asks you, 'Why did you get so close to the city to fight? Didn't you realize they would shoot from the top of the wall? ²¹ At Thebez, who struck Abimelech son of Jerubbesheth? Didn't a woman drop an upper millstone on him

from the top of the wall so that he died? Why did you get so close to the wall?' — then say, 'Your servant Uriah the Hethite is dead also.' " ²² Then the messenger left.

When he arrived, he reported to David all that Joab had sent him to tell. ²³ The messenger reported to David, "The men gained the advantage over us and came out against us in the field, but we counterattacked right up to the entrance of the city gate. ²⁴ However, the archers shot down on your servants from the top of the wall, and some of the king's servants died. Your servant Uriah the Hethite is also dead."

²⁵ David told the messenger, "Say this to Joab: 'Don't let this matter upset you because the sword devours all alike. Intensify your fight against the city and demolish it.' Encourage him."

²⁶ When Uriah's wife heard that her husband, Uriah, had died, she mourned for him. ²⁷ When the time of mourning ended, David had her brought to his house. She became his wife and bore him a son. However, the LORD considered what David had done to be evil.

Nathan's Parable and David's Repentance

12 So the LORD sent Nathan to David. When he arrived, he said to him:

There were two men in a certain city, one rich and the other poor. ² The rich man had very large flocks and herds, ³ but the poor man had nothing except one small ewe lamb that he had bought. He raised her, and she grew up with him and with his children. From his meager food she would eat, from his cup she would drink, and in his arms she would sleep. She was like a daughter to him. ⁴ Now a traveler came to the rich man, but the rich man could not bring himself to take one of his own sheep or cattle to prepare for the traveler who had come to him. Instead, he took the poor man's lamb and prepared it for his guest.

⁵ David was infuriated with the man and said to Nathan, "As the LORD lives, the man who did this deserves to die! ⁶ Because he has done this thing and shown no pity, he must pay four lambs for that lamb."

⁷ Nathan replied to David, "You are the man! This is what the LORD God of Israel says: 'I anointed you king over Israel, and I rescued you from Saul. ⁸ I gave your master's house to you and your master's wives into your arms, and I gave you the house of Israel and Judah, and if that was not enough, I would have given you even more. ⁹ Why then have you despised the LORD's command by doing what I consider evil? You struck down Uriah the Hethite with the sword and took his wife as your own wife — you murdered him with the Ammonite's sword. ¹⁰ Now therefore, the sword will never leave your house because you despised me and took the wife of Uriah the Hethite to be your own wife.'

¹¹ "This is what the LORD says, 'I am going to bring disaster on you from your own family: I will take your wives and give them to another before your very eyes, and he will sleep with them in broad daylight. ¹² You acted in secret, but I will do this before all Israel and in broad daylight.'"

¹³ David responded to Nathan, "I have sinned against the LORD."

Then Nathan replied to David, "And the LORD has taken away your sin; you will not die. ¹⁴ However, because you treated the LORD with such contempt in this matter, the son born to you will die." ¹⁵ Then Nathan went home.

The Death of Bathsheba's Son
The LORD struck the baby that Uriah's wife had borne to David, and he became deathly ill. ¹⁶ David pleaded with God for the boy. He fasted, went home, and spent the night lying on the ground. ¹⁷ The elders of his house stood beside him to get him

up from the ground, but he was unwilling and would not eat anything with them.

¹⁸ On the seventh day the baby died. But David's servants were afraid to tell him the baby was dead. They said, "Look, while the baby was alive, we spoke to him, and he wouldn't listen to us. So how can we tell him the baby is dead? He may do something desperate."

¹⁹ When David saw that his servants were whispering to each other, he guessed that the baby was dead. So he asked his servants, "Is the baby dead?"

"He is dead," they replied.

²⁰ Then David got up from the ground. He washed, anointed himself, changed his clothes, went to the LORD's house, and worshiped. Then he went home and requested something to eat. So they served him food, and he ate.

²¹ His servants asked him, "Why have you done this? While the baby was alive, you fasted and wept, but when he died, you got up and ate food."

²² He answered, "While the baby was alive, I fasted and wept because I thought, 'Who knows? The LORD may be gracious to me and let him live.' ²³ But now that he is dead, why should I fast? Can I bring him back again? I'll go to him, but he will never return to me."

The Birth of Solomon
²⁴ Then David comforted his wife Bathsheba; he went to her and slept with her. She gave birth to a son and named him Solomon. The LORD loved him, ²⁵ and he sent a message through the prophet Nathan, who named him Jedidiah, because of the LORD.

Capture of the City of Rabbah
²⁶ Joab fought against Rabbah of the Ammonites and captured the royal fortress. ²⁷ Then Joab sent messengers to David to say,

"I have fought against Rabbah and have also captured its water supply. ²⁸ Now therefore, assemble the rest of the troops, lay siege to the city, and capture it. Otherwise I will be the one to capture the city, and it will be named after me." ²⁹ So David assembled all the troops and went to Rabbah; he fought against it and captured it. ³⁰ He took the crown from the head of their king, and it was placed on David's head. The crown weighed seventy-five pounds of gold, and it had a precious stone in it. In addition, David took away a large quantity of plunder from the city. ³¹ He removed the people who were in the city and put them to work with saws, iron picks, and iron axes, and to labor at brickmaking. He did the same to all the Ammonite cities. Then he and all his troops returned to Jerusalem.

Amnon Rapes Tamar

13 Some time passed. David's son Absalom had a beautiful sister named Tamar, and David's son Amnon was infatuated with her. ² Amnon was frustrated to the point of making himself sick over his sister Tamar because she was a virgin, but it seemed impossible to do anything to her. ³ Amnon had a friend named Jonadab, a son of David's brother Shimeah. Jonadab was a very shrewd man, ⁴ and he asked Amnon, "Why are you, the king's son, so miserable every morning? Won't you tell me?"

Amnon replied, "I'm in love with Tamar, my brother Absalom's sister."

⁵ Jonadab said to him, "Lie down on your bed and pretend you're sick. When your father comes to see you, say to him, 'Please let my sister Tamar come and give me something to eat. Let her prepare a meal in my presence so I can watch and eat from her hand.'"

⁶ So Amnon lay down and pretended to be sick. When the king came to see him, Amnon said to him, "Please let my sister

Tamar come and make a couple of cakes in my presence so I can eat from her hand."

⁷ David sent word to Tamar at the palace: "Please go to your brother Amnon's house and prepare a meal for him."

⁸ Then Tamar went to his house while Amnon was lying down. She took dough, kneaded it, made cakes in his presence, and baked them. ⁹ She brought the pan and set it down in front of him, but he refused to eat. Amnon said, "Everyone leave me!" And everyone left him. ¹⁰ "Bring the meal to the bedroom," Amnon told Tamar, "so I can eat from your hand." Tamar took the cakes she had made and went to her brother Amnon's bedroom. ¹¹ When she brought them to him to eat, he grabbed her and said, "Come sleep with me, my sister!"

¹² "Don't, my brother!" she cried. "Don't disgrace me, for such a thing should never be done in Israel. Don't commit this outrage! ¹³ Where could I ever go with my humiliation? And you — you would be like one of the outrageous fools in Israel! Please, speak to the king, for he won't keep me from you." ¹⁴ But he refused to listen to her, and because he was stronger than she was, he disgraced her by raping her.

¹⁵ So Amnon hated Tamar with such intensity that the hatred he hated her with was greater than the love he had loved her with. "Get out of here!" he said.

¹⁶ "No," she cried, "sending me away is much worse than the great wrong you've already done to me!"

But he refused to listen to her. ¹⁷ Instead, he called to the servant who waited on him, "Get this away from me, throw her out, and bolt the door behind her!" ¹⁸ Amnon's servant threw her out and bolted the door behind her. Now Tamar was wearing a long-sleeved robe, because this is what the king's virgin daughters wore. ¹⁹ Tamar put ashes on her head and tore the long-sleeved robe she was wearing. She put her hand on her head and went away crying out.

²⁰ Her brother Absalom said to her, "Has your brother Amnon been with you? Be quiet for now, my sister. He is your brother. Don't take this thing to heart." So Tamar lived as a desolate woman in the house of her brother Absalom.

Absalom Murders Amnon

²¹ When King David heard about all these things, he was furious. ²² Absalom didn't say anything to Amnon, either good or bad, because he hated Amnon since he disgraced his sister Tamar.

²³ Two years later, Absalom's sheepshearers were at Baalhazor near Ephraim, and Absalom invited all the king's sons. ²⁴ Then he went to the king and said, "Your servant has just hired sheepshearers. Will the king and his servants please come with your servant?"

²⁵ The king replied to Absalom, "No, my son, we should not all go, or we would be a burden to you." Although Absalom urged him, he wasn't willing to go, though he did bless him.

²⁶ "If not," Absalom said, "please let my brother Amnon go with us."

The king asked him, "Why should he go with you?" ²⁷ But Absalom urged him, so he sent Amnon and all the king's sons.

²⁸ Now Absalom commanded his young men, "Watch Amnon until he is in a good mood from the wine. When I order you to strike Amnon, then kill him. Don't be afraid. Am I not the one who has commanded you? Be strong and valiant!" ²⁹ So Absalom's young men did to Amnon just as Absalom had commanded. Then all the rest of the king's sons got up, and each fled on his mule.

³⁰ While they were on the way, a report reached David: "Absalom struck down all the king's sons; not even one of them survived!" ³¹ In response the king stood up, tore his clothes, and lay down on the ground, and all his servants stood by with their clothes torn.

³²But Jonadab, son of David's brother Shimeah, spoke up: "My lord must not think they have killed all the young men, the king's sons, because only Amnon is dead. In fact, Absalom has planned this ever since the day Amnon disgraced his sister Tamar. ³³So now, my lord the king, don't take seriously the report that says all the king's sons are dead. Only Amnon is dead."

³⁴Meanwhile, Absalom had fled. When the young man who was standing watch looked up, there were many people coming from the road west of him from the side of the mountain. ³⁵Jonadab said to the king, "Look, the king's sons have come! It's exactly like your servant said." ³⁶Just as he finished speaking, the king's sons entered and wept loudly. Then the king and all his servants also wept very bitterly. ³⁷But Absalom fled and went to Talmai son of Ammihud, king of Geshur. And David mourned for his son every day.

³⁸After Absalom had fled to Geshur and had been there three years, ³⁹King David longed to go to Absalom, for David had finished grieving over Amnon's death.

Absalom Restored to David

14 Joab son of Zeruiah realized that the king's mind was on Absalom. ²So Joab sent someone to Tekoa to bring a wise woman from there. He told her, "Pretend to be in mourning: dress in mourning clothes and don't put on any oil. Act like a woman who has been mourning for the dead for a long time. ³Go to the king and speak these words to him." Then Joab told her exactly what to say.

⁴When the woman from Tekoa came to the king, she fell facedown to the ground, paid homage, and said, "Help me, Your Majesty!"

⁵"What's the matter?" the king asked her.

"Sadly, I am a widow; my husband died," she said. ⁶"Your servant had two sons. They were fighting in the field with no

one to separate them, and one struck the other and killed him. ⁷Now the whole clan has risen up against your servant and said, 'Hand over the one who killed his brother so we may put him to death for the life of the brother he murdered. We will eliminate the heir!' They would extinguish my one remaining ember by not preserving my husband's name or posterity on earth."

⁸The king told the woman, "Go home. I will issue a command on your behalf."

⁹Then the woman of Tekoa said to the king, "My lord the king, may any blame be on me and my father's family, and may the king and his throne be innocent."

¹⁰"Whoever speaks to you," the king said, "bring him to me. He will not trouble you again!"

¹¹She replied, "Please, may the king invoke the LORD your God, so that the avenger of blood will not increase the loss, and they will not eliminate my son!"

"As the LORD lives," he vowed, "not a hair of your son will fall to the ground."

¹²Then the woman said, "Please, may your servant speak a word to my lord the king?"

"Speak," he replied.

¹³The woman asked, "Why have you devised something similar against the people of God? When the king spoke as he did about this matter, he has pronounced his own guilt. The king has not brought back his own banished one. ¹⁴We will certainly die and be like water poured out on the ground, which can't be recovered. But God would not take away a life; he would devise plans so that the one banished from him does not remain banished.

¹⁵"Now therefore, I've come to present this matter to my lord the king because the people have made me afraid. Your servant thought: I must speak to the king. Perhaps the king will grant

his servant's request. ¹⁶ The king will surely listen in order to keep his servant from the grasp of this man who would eliminate both me and my son from God's inheritance. ¹⁷ Your servant thought: May the word of my lord the king bring relief, for my lord the king is able to discern the good and the bad like the angel of God. May the LORD your God be with you."

¹⁸ Then the king answered the woman, "I'm going to ask you something; don't conceal it from me!"

"Let my lord the king speak," the woman replied.

¹⁹ The king asked, "Did Joab put you up to all this?"

The woman answered. "As you live, my lord the king, no one can turn to the right or left from all my lord the king says. Yes, your servant Joab is the one who gave orders to me; he told your servant exactly what to say. ²⁰ Joab your servant has done this to address the issue indirectly, but my lord has wisdom like the wisdom of the angel of God, knowing everything on earth."

²¹ Then the king said to Joab, "I hereby grant this request. Go, bring back the young man Absalom."

²² Joab fell with his face to the ground in homage and blessed the king. "Today," Joab said, "your servant knows I have found favor with you, my lord the king, because the king has granted the request of your servant."

²³ So Joab got up, went to Geshur, and brought Absalom to Jerusalem. ²⁴ However, the king added, "He may return to his house, but he may not see my face." So Absalom returned to his house, but he did not see the king.

²⁵ No man in all Israel was as handsome and highly praised as Absalom. From the sole of his foot to the top of his head, he did not have a single flaw. ²⁶ When he shaved his head — he shaved it at the end of every year because his hair got so heavy for him that he had to shave it off — he would weigh the hair from his head and it would be five pounds according to the royal standard.

²⁷ Three sons were born to Absalom, and a daughter named Tamar, who was a beautiful woman. ²⁸ Absalom resided in Jerusalem two years but never saw the king. ²⁹ Then Absalom sent for Joab in order to send him to the king, but Joab was unwilling to come to him. So he sent again, a second time, but he still would not come. ³⁰ Then Absalom said to his servants, "See, Joab has a field right next to mine, and he has barley there. Go and set fire to it!" So Absalom's servants set the field on fire.

³¹ Then Joab came to Absalom's house and demanded, "Why did your servants set my field on fire?"

³² "Look," Absalom explained to Joab, "I sent for you and said, 'Come here. I want to send you to the king to ask: Why have I come back from Geshur? I'd be better off if I were still there.' So now, let me see the king. If I am guilty, let him kill me."

³³ Joab went to the king and told him. So David summoned Absalom, who came to the king and paid homage with his face to the ground before him. Then the king kissed Absalom.

Absalom's Revolt

15 After this, Absalom got himself a chariot, horses, and fifty men to run before him. ² He would get up early and stand beside the road leading to the city gate. Whenever anyone had a grievance to bring before the king for settlement, Absalom called out to him and asked, "What city are you from?" If he replied, "Your servant is from one of the tribes of Israel," ³ Absalom said to him, "Look, your claims are good and right, but the king does not have anyone to listen to you." ⁴ He added, "If only someone would appoint me judge in the land. Then anyone who had a grievance or dispute could come to me, and I would make sure he received justice." ⁵ When a person approached to pay homage to him, Absalom reached out his hand, took hold of him, and kissed him. ⁶ Absalom did this to all the Israelites who came to the king for a settlement. So Absalom stole the hearts of the men of Israel.

⁷When four years had passed, Absalom said to the king, "Please let me go to Hebron to fulfill a vow I made to the LORD. ⁸For your servant made a vow when I lived in Geshur of Aram, saying, 'If the LORD really brings me back to Jerusalem, I will worship the LORD in Hebron.'"

⁹"Go in peace," the king said to him. So he went to Hebron.

¹⁰Then Absalom sent agents throughout the tribes of Israel with this message: "When you hear the sound of the ram's horn, you are to say, 'Absalom has become king in Hebron!'"

¹¹Two hundred men from Jerusalem went with Absalom. They had been invited and were going innocently, for they did not know the whole situation. ¹²While he was offering the sacrifices, Absalom sent for David's adviser Ahithophel the Gilonite, from his city of Giloh. So the conspiracy grew strong, and the people supporting Absalom continued to increase.

¹³Then an informer came to David and reported, "The hearts of the men of Israel are with Absalom."

¹⁴David said to all the servants with him in Jerusalem, "Get up. We have to flee, or we will not escape from Absalom! Leave quickly, or he will overtake us quickly, heap disaster on us, and strike the city with the edge of the sword."

¹⁵The king's servants said to the king, "Whatever my lord the king decides, we are your servants." ¹⁶Then the king set out, and his entire household followed him. But he left behind ten concubines to take care of the palace. ¹⁷So the king set out, and all the people followed him. They stopped at the last house ¹⁸while all his servants marched past him. Then all the Cherethites, the Pelethites, and the people of Gath—six hundred men who came with him from there—marched past the king.

¹⁹The king said to Ittai of Gath, "Why are you also going with us? Go back and stay with the new king since you're both a foreigner and an exile from your homeland. ²⁰Besides, you only arrived yesterday; should I make you wander around with us

today while I go wherever I can? Go back and take your brothers with you. May the LORD show you kindness and faithfulness."

²¹ But in response, Ittai vowed to the king, "As the LORD lives and as my lord the king lives, wherever my lord the king is, whether it means life or death, your servant will be there!"

²² "March on," David replied to Ittai. So Ittai of Gath marched past with all his men and the dependents who were with him. ²³ Everyone in the countryside was weeping loudly while all the people were marching out of the city. As the king was crossing the Kidron Valley, all the people were marching past on the road that leads to the wilderness.

²⁴ Zadok was also there, and all the Levites with him were carrying the ark of the covenant of God. They set the ark of God down, and Abiathar offered sacrifices until the people had finished marching past. ²⁵ Then the king instructed Zadok, "Return the ark of God to the city. If I find favor with the LORD, he will bring me back and allow me to see both it and its dwelling place. ²⁶ However, if he should say, 'I do not delight in you,' then here I am — he can do with me whatever pleases him."

²⁷ The king also said to the priest Zadok, "Look, return to the city in peace and your two sons with you: your son Ahimaaz and Abiathar's son Jonathan. ²⁸ Remember, I'll wait at the fords of the wilderness until word comes from you to inform me." ²⁹ So Zadok and Abiathar returned the ark of God to Jerusalem and stayed there.

³⁰ David was climbing the slope of the Mount of Olives, weeping as he ascended. His head was covered, and he was walking barefoot. All of the people with him covered their heads and went up, weeping as they ascended.

³¹ Then someone reported to David, "Ahithophel is among the conspirators with Absalom."

"LORD," David pleaded, "please turn the counsel of Ahithophel into foolishness!"

³² When David came to the summit where he used to worship God, Hushai the Archite was there to meet him with his robe torn and dust on his head. ³³ David said to him, "If you go away with me, you'll be a burden to me, ³⁴ but if you return to the city and tell Absalom, 'I will be your servant, Your Majesty! Previously, I was your father's servant, but now I will be your servant,' then you can counteract Ahithophel's counsel for me. ³⁵ Won't the priests Zadok and Abiathar be there with you? Report everything you hear from the palace to the priests Zadok and Abiathar. ³⁶ Take note: their two sons are there with them—Zadok's son Ahimaaz and Abiathar's son Jonathan. Send them to tell me everything you hear." ³⁷ So Hushai, David's personal adviser, entered Jerusalem just as Absalom was entering the city.

Ziba Helps David

16 When David had gone a little beyond the summit, Ziba, Mephibosheth's servant, was right there to meet him. He had a pair of saddled donkeys loaded with two hundred loaves of bread, one hundred clusters of raisins, one hundred bunches of summer fruit, and a clay jar of wine. ² The king said to Ziba, "Why do you have these?"

Ziba answered, "The donkeys are for the king's household to ride, the bread and summer fruit are for the young men to eat, and the wine is for those to drink who become exhausted in the wilderness."

³ "Where is your master's grandson?" the king asked.

"Why, he's staying in Jerusalem," Ziba replied to the king, "for he said, 'Today, the house of Israel will restore my grandfather's kingdom to me.'"

⁴ The king said to Ziba, "All that belongs to Mephibosheth is now yours!"

"I bow before you," Ziba said. "May I find favor with you, my lord the king!"

Shimei Curses David

⁵ When King David got to Bahurim, a man belonging to the family of the house of Saul was just coming out. His name was Shimei son of Gera, and he was yelling curses as he approached. ⁶ He threw stones at David and at all the royal servants, the people and the warriors on David's right and left. ⁷ Shimei said as he cursed, "Get out, get out, you man of bloodshed, you wicked man! ⁸ The LORD has paid you back for all the blood of the house of Saul in whose place you became king, and the LORD has handed the kingdom over to your son Absalom. Look, you are in trouble because you're a man of bloodshed!"

⁹ Then Abishai son of Zeruiah said to the king, "Why should this dead dog curse my lord the king? Let me go over and remove his head!"

¹⁰ The king replied, "Sons of Zeruiah, do we agree on anything? He curses me this way because the LORD told him, 'Curse David!' Therefore, who can say, 'Why did you do that?'" ¹¹ Then David said to Abishai and all his servants, "Look, my own son, my own flesh and blood, intends to take my life — how much more now this Benjaminite! Leave him alone and let him curse me; the LORD has told him to. ¹² Perhaps the LORD will see my affliction and restore goodness to me instead of Shimei's curses today." ¹³ So David and his men proceeded along the road as Shimei was going along the ridge of the hill opposite him. As Shimei went, he cursed David, threw stones at him, and kicked up dust. ¹⁴ Finally, the king and all the people with him arrived exhausted, so they rested there.

Absalom's Advisers

¹⁵ Now Absalom and all the Israelites came to Jerusalem. Ahithophel was also with him. ¹⁶ When David's friend Hushai the Archite came to Absalom, Hushai said to Absalom, "Long live the king! Long live the king!"

¹⁷ "Is this your loyalty to your friend?" Absalom asked Hushai. "Why didn't you go with your friend?"

¹⁸ "Not at all," Hushai answered Absalom. "I am on the side of the one that the LORD, this people, and all the men of Israel have chosen. I will stay with him. ¹⁹ Furthermore, whom will I serve if not his son? As I served in your father's presence, I will also serve in yours."

²⁰ Then Absalom said to Ahithophel, "Give me your advice. What should we do?"

²¹ Ahithophel replied to Absalom, "Sleep with your father's concubines whom he left to take care of the palace. When all Israel hears that you have become repulsive to your father, everyone with you will be encouraged." ²² So they pitched a tent for Absalom on the roof, and he slept with his father's concubines in the sight of all Israel.

²³ Now the advice Ahithophel gave in those days was like someone asking about a word from God — such was the regard that both David and Absalom had for Ahithophel's advice.

17 ¹ Ahithophel said to Absalom, "Let me choose twelve thousand men, and I will set out in pursuit of David tonight. ² I will attack him while he is weary and discouraged, throw him into a panic, and all the people with him will scatter. I will strike down only the king ³ and bring all the people back to you. When everyone returns except the man you're looking for, all the people will be at peace." ⁴ This proposal seemed right to Absalom and all the elders of Israel.

⁵ Then Absalom said, "Summon Hushai the Archite also. Let's hear what he has to say as well."

⁶ So Hushai came to Absalom, and Absalom told him, "Ahithophel offered this proposal. Should we carry out his proposal? If not, what do you say?"

⁷ Hushai replied to Absalom, "The advice Ahithophel has given this time is not good." ⁸ Hushai continued, "You know your

father and his men. They are warriors and are desperate like a wild bear robbed of her cubs. Your father is an experienced soldier who won't spend the night with the people. [9] He's probably already hiding in one of the caves or some other place. If some of our troops fall first, someone is sure to hear and say, 'There's been a slaughter among the people who follow Absalom.' [10] Then, even a brave man with the heart of a lion will lose heart because all Israel knows that your father and the valiant men with him are warriors. [11] Instead, I advise that all Israel from Dan to Beer-sheba — as numerous as the sand by the sea — be gathered to you and that you personally go into battle. [12] Then we will attack David wherever we find him, and we will descend on him like dew on the ground. Not even one will be left—neither he nor any of the men with him. [13] If he retreats to some city, all Israel will bring ropes to that city, and we will drag its stones into the valley until not even a pebble can be found there." [14] Since the LORD had decreed that Ahithophel's good advice be undermined in order to bring about Absalom's ruin, Absalom and all the men of Israel said, "The advice of Hushai the Archite is better than Ahithophel's advice."

David Informed of Absalom's Plans

[15] Hushai then told the priests Zadok and Abiathar, "This is what Ahithophel advised Absalom and the elders of Israel, and this is what I advised. [16] Now send someone quickly and tell David, 'Don't spend the night at the wilderness ford, but be sure to cross over the Jordan, or the king and all the people with him will be devoured.'"

[17] Jonathan and Ahimaaz were staying at En-rogel, where a servant girl would come and pass along information to them. They in turn would go and inform King David, because they dared not be seen entering the city. [18] However, a young man did see them and informed Absalom. So the two left quickly

and came to the house of a man in Bahurim. He had a well in his courtyard, and they climbed down into it. **19** Then his wife took the cover, placed it over the mouth of the well, and scattered grain on it so nobody would know anything.

20 Absalom's servants came to the woman at the house and asked, "Where are Ahimaaz and Jonathan?"

"They passed by toward the water," the woman replied to them. The men searched but did not find them, so they returned to Jerusalem.

21 After they had gone, Ahimaaz and Jonathan climbed out of the well and went and informed King David. They told him, "Get up and immediately ford the river, for Ahithophel has given this advice against you." **22** So David and all the people with him got up and crossed the Jordan. By daybreak, there was no one who had not crossed the Jordan.

23 When Ahithophel realized that his advice had not been followed, he saddled his donkey and set out for his house in his hometown. He set his house in order and hanged himself. So he died and was buried in his father's tomb.

24 David had arrived at Mahanaim by the time Absalom crossed the Jordan with all the men of Israel. **25** Now Absalom had appointed Amasa over the army in Joab's place. Amasa was the son of a man named Ithra the Israelite; Ithra had married Abigail daughter of Nahash. Abigail was a sister to Zeruiah, Joab's mother. **26** And Israel and Absalom camped in the land of Gilead. **27** When David came to Mahanaim, Shobi son of Nahash from Rabbah of the Ammonites, Machir son of Ammiel from Lo-debar, and Barzillai the Gileadite from Rogelim **28** brought beds, basins, and pottery items. They also brought wheat, barley, flour, roasted grain, beans, lentils, **29** honey, curds, sheep, goats, and cheese from the herd for David and the people with him to eat. They had reasoned, "The people must be hungry, exhausted, and thirsty in the wilderness."

Absalom's Defeat

18 David reviewed his troops and appointed commanders of thousands and of hundreds over them. ² He then sent out the troops, a third under Joab, a third under Joab's brother Abishai son of Zeruiah, and a third under Ittai of Gath. The king said to the troops, "I must also march out with you."

³ "You must not go!" the people pleaded. "If we have to flee, they will not pay any attention to us. Even if half of us die, they will not pay any attention to us because you are worth ten thousand of us. Therefore, it is better if you support us from the city."

⁴ "I will do whatever you think is best," the king replied to them. So he stood beside the city gate while all the troops marched out by hundreds and thousands. ⁵ The king commanded Joab, Abishai, and Ittai, "Treat the young man Absalom gently for my sake." All the people heard the king's orders to all the commanders about Absalom.

⁶ Then David's forces marched into the field to engage Israel in battle, which took place in the forest of Ephraim. ⁷ Israel's army was defeated by David's soldiers, and the slaughter there was vast that day — twenty thousand dead. ⁸ The battle spread over the entire area, and that day the forest claimed more people than the sword.

Absalom's Death

⁹ Absalom was riding on his mule when he happened to meet David's soldiers. When the mule went under the tangled branches of a large oak tree, Absalom's head was caught fast in the tree. The mule under him kept going, so he was suspended in midair. ¹⁰ One of the men saw him and informed Joab. He said, "I just saw Absalom hanging in an oak tree!"

¹¹ "You just saw him!" Joab exclaimed. "Why didn't you strike him to the ground right there? I would have given you ten silver pieces and a belt!"

¹² The man replied to Joab, "Even if I had the weight of a thousand pieces of silver in my hand, I would not raise my hand against the king's son. For we heard the king command you, Abishai, and Ittai, 'Protect the young man Absalom for me.' ¹³ If I had jeopardized my own life — and nothing is hidden from the king — you would have abandoned me."

¹⁴ Joab said, "I'm not going to waste time with you!" He then took three spears in his hand and thrust them into Absalom's chest. While Absalom was still alive in the oak tree, ¹⁵ ten young men who were Joab's armor-bearers surrounded Absalom, struck him, and killed him. ¹⁶ Joab blew the ram's horn, and the troops broke off their pursuit of Israel because Joab restrained them. ¹⁷ They took Absalom, threw him into a large pit in the forest, and raised up a huge mound of stones over him. And all Israel fled, each to his tent.

¹⁸ When he was alive, Absalom had taken a pillar and raised it up for himself in the King's Valley, since he thought, "I have no son to preserve the memory of my name." So he named the pillar after himself. It is still called Absalom's Monument today.

¹⁹ Ahimaaz son of Zadok said, "Please let me run and tell the king the good news that the LORD has vindicated him by freeing him from his enemies."

²⁰ Joab replied to him, "You are not the man to take good news today. You may do it another day, but today you aren't taking good news, because the king's son is dead." ²¹ Joab then said to a Cushite, "Go tell the king what you have seen." The Cushite bowed to Joab and took off running.

²² However, Ahimaaz son of Zadok persisted and said to Joab, "No matter what, please let me also run behind the Cushite!"

Joab replied, "My son, why do you want to run since you won't get a reward?"

²³ "No matter what, I want to run!"

"Then run!" Joab said to him. So Ahimaaz ran by way of the plain and outran the Cushite.

²⁴ David was sitting between the city gates when the watchman went up to the roof of the city gate and over to the wall. The watchman looked out and saw a man running alone. ²⁵ He called out and told the king.

The king said, "If he's alone, he bears good news."

As the first runner came closer, ²⁶ the watchman saw another man running. He called out to the gatekeeper, "Look! Another man is running alone!"

"This one is also bringing good news," said the king.

²⁷ The watchman said, "The way the first man runs looks to me like the way Ahimaaz son of Zadok runs."

"This is a good man; he comes with good news," the king commented.

²⁸ Ahimaaz called out to the king, "All is well," and paid homage to the king with his face to the ground. He continued, "Blessed be the LORD your God! He delivered up the men who rebelled against my lord the king."

²⁹ The king asked, "Is the young man Absalom all right?"

Ahimaaz replied, "When Joab sent the king's servant and your servant, I saw a big disturbance, but I don't know what it was."

³⁰ The king said, "Move aside and stand here." So he stood to one side.

³¹ Just then the Cushite came and said, "May my lord the king hear the good news: The LORD has vindicated you today by freeing you from all who rise against you!"

³² The king asked the Cushite, "Is the young man Absalom all right?"

The Cushite replied, "I wish that the enemies of my lord the king, along with all who rise up against you with evil intent, would become like that young man."

³³ The king was deeply moved and went up to the chamber above the city gate and wept. As he walked, he cried, "My son Absalom! My son, my son Absalom! If only I had died instead of you, Absalom, my son, my son!"

David's Kingdom Restored

19 It was reported to Joab, "The king is weeping. He's mourning over Absalom." ² That day's victory was turned into mourning for all the troops because on that day the troops heard, "The king is grieving over his son." ³ So they returned to the city quietly that day like troops come in when they are humiliated after fleeing in battle. ⁴ But the king covered his face and cried loudly, "My son Absalom! Absalom, my son, my son!"

⁵ Then Joab went into the house to the king and said, "Today you have shamed all your soldiers — those who saved your life as well as your sons, your wives, and your concubines — ⁶ by loving your enemies and hating those who love you! Today you have made it clear that the commanders and soldiers mean nothing to you. In fact, today I know that if Absalom were alive and all of us were dead, it would be fine with you!

⁷ "Now get up! Go out and encourage your soldiers, for I swear by the LORD that if you don't go out, not a man will remain with you tonight. This will be worse for you than all the trouble that has come to you from your youth until now!"

⁸ So the king got up and sat in the city gate, and all the people were told, "Look, the king is sitting in the city gate." Then they all came into the king's presence.

Meanwhile, each Israelite had fled to his tent. ⁹ People throughout all the tribes of Israel were arguing among themselves, saying, "The king rescued us from the grasp of our enemies, and he saved us from the grasp of the Philistines, but now he has fled from the land because of Absalom. ¹⁰ But Absalom,

the man we anointed over us, has died in battle. So why do you say nothing about restoring the king?"

¹¹ King David sent word to the priests Zadok and Abiathar: "Say to the elders of Judah, 'Why should you be the last to restore the king to his palace? The talk of all Israel has reached the king at his house. ¹² You are my brothers, my flesh and blood. So why should you be the last to restore the king?' ¹³ And tell Amasa, 'Aren't you my flesh and blood? May God punish me and do so severely if you don't become commander of my army from now on instead of Joab!'"

¹⁴ So he won over all the men of Judah, and they unanimously sent word to the king: "Come back, you and all your servants." ¹⁵ Then the king returned. When he arrived at the Jordan, Judah came to Gilgal to meet the king and escort him across the Jordan.

¹⁶ Shimei son of Gera, the Benjaminite from Bahurim, hurried down with the men of Judah to meet King David. ¹⁷ There were a thousand men from Benjamin with him. Ziba, an attendant from the house of Saul, with his fifteen sons and twenty servants also rushed down to the Jordan ahead of the king. ¹⁸ They forded the Jordan to bring the king's household across and do whatever the king desired.

When Shimei son of Gera crossed the Jordan, he fell facedown before the king ¹⁹ and said to him, "My lord, don't hold me guilty, and don't remember your servant's wrongdoing on the day my lord the king left Jerusalem. May the king not take it to heart. ²⁰ For your servant knows that I have sinned. But look! Today I am the first one of the entire house of Joseph to come down to meet my lord the king."

²¹ Abishai son of Zeruiah asked, "Shouldn't Shimei be put to death for this, because he cursed the LORD's anointed?"

²² David answered, "Sons of Zeruiah, do we agree on anything? Have you become my adversary today? Should any man

be killed in Israel today? Am I not aware that today I'm king over Israel?" ²³ So the king said to Shimei, "You will not die." Then the king gave him his oath.

²⁴ Mephibosheth, Saul's grandson, also went down to meet the king. He had not taken care of his feet, trimmed his mustache, or washed his clothes from the day the king left until the day he returned safely. ²⁵ When he came from Jerusalem to meet the king, the king asked him, "Mephibosheth, why didn't you come with me?"

²⁶ "My lord the king," he replied, "my servant Ziba betrayed me. Actually your servant said, 'I'll saddle the donkey for myself so that I may ride it and go with the king' — for your servant is lame. ²⁷ Ziba slandered your servant to my lord the king. But my lord the king is like the angel of God, so do whatever you think best. ²⁸ For my grandfather's entire family deserves death from my lord the king, but you set your servant among those who eat at your table. So what further right do I have to keep on making appeals to the king?"

²⁹ The king said to him, "Why keep on speaking about these matters of yours? I hereby declare: you and Ziba are to divide the land."

³⁰ Mephibosheth said to the king, "Instead, since my lord the king has come to his palace safely, let Ziba take it all!"

³¹ Barzillai the Gileadite had come down from Rogelim and accompanied the king to the Jordan River to see him off at the Jordan. ³² Barzillai was a very old man — eighty years old — and since he was a very wealthy man, he had provided for the needs of the king while he stayed in Mahanaim.

³³ The king said to Barzillai, "Cross over with me, and I'll provide for you at my side in Jerusalem."

³⁴ Barzillai replied to the king, "How many years of my life are left that I should go up to Jerusalem with the king? ³⁵ I'm now eighty years old. Can I discern what is pleasant and what is not?

Can your servant taste what he eats or drinks? Can I still hear the voice of male and female singers? Why should your servant be an added burden to my lord the king? ³⁶ Since your servant is only going with the king a little way across the Jordan, why should the king repay me with such a reward? ³⁷ Please let your servant return so that I may die in my own city near the tomb of my father and mother. But here is your servant Chimham; let him cross over with my lord the king. Do for him what seems good to you."

³⁸ The king replied, "Chimham will cross over with me, and I will do for him what seems good to you, and whatever you desire from me I will do for you." ³⁹ So all the people crossed the Jordan, and then the king crossed. The king kissed Barzillai and blessed him, and Barzillai returned to his home.

⁴⁰ The king went on to Gilgal, and Chimham went with him. All the troops of Judah and half of Israel's escorted the king. ⁴¹ Suddenly, all the men of Israel came to the king. They asked him, "Why did our brothers, the men of Judah, take you away secretly and transport the king and his household across the Jordan, along with all of David's men?"

⁴² All the men of Judah responded to the men of Israel, "Because the king is our relative. Why does this make you angry? Have we ever eaten anything of the king's or been honored at all?"

⁴³ The men of Israel answered the men of Judah, "We have ten shares in the king, so we have a greater claim to David than you. Why then do you despise us? Weren't we the first to speak of restoring our king?" But the words of the men of Judah were harsher than those of the men of Israel.

Sheba's Revolt

20 Now a wicked man, a Benjaminite named Sheba son of Bichri, happened to be there. He blew the ram's horn and shouted:

We have no portion in David,
no inheritance in Jesse's son.

Each man to his tent, Israel!

² So all the men of Israel deserted David and followed Sheba son of Bichri, but the men of Judah from the Jordan all the way to Jerusalem remained loyal to their king.

³ When David came to his palace in Jerusalem, he took the ten concubines he had left to take care of the palace and placed them under guard. He provided for them, but he was not intimate with them. They were confined until the day of their death, living as widows.

⁴ The king said to Amasa, "Summon the men of Judah to me within three days and be here yourself." ⁵ Amasa went to summon Judah, but he took longer than the time allotted him. ⁶ So David said to Abishai, "Sheba son of Bichri will do more harm to us than Absalom. Take your lord's soldiers and pursue him, or he will find fortified cities and elude us."

⁷ So Joab's men, the Cherethites, the Pelethites, and all the warriors marched out under Abishai's command; they left Jerusalem to pursue Sheba son of Bichri. ⁸ They were at the great stone in Gibeon when Amasa joined them. Joab was wearing his uniform and over it was a belt around his waist with a sword in its sheath. As he approached, the sword fell out. ⁹ Joab asked Amasa, "Are you well, my brother?" Then with his right hand Joab grabbed Amasa by the beard to kiss him. ¹⁰ Amasa was not on guard against the sword in Joab's hand, and Joab stabbed him in the stomach with it and spilled his intestines out on the ground. Joab did not stab him again, and Amasa died.

Joab and his brother Abishai pursued Sheba son of Bichri. ¹¹ One of Joab's young men had stood over Amasa saying, "Whoever favors Joab and whoever is for David, follow Joab!" ¹² Now Amasa had been writhing in his blood in the middle of

the highway, and the man had seen that all the troops stopped. So he moved Amasa from the highway to the field and threw a garment over him because he realized that all those who encountered Amasa were stopping. ¹³ When he was removed from the highway, all the men passed by and followed Joab to pursue Sheba son of Bichri.

¹⁴ Sheba passed through all the tribes of Israel to Abel of Beth-maacah. All the Berites came together and followed him. ¹⁵ Joab's troops came and besieged Sheba in Abel of Beth-maacah. They built a siege ramp against the outer wall of the city. While all the troops with Joab were battering the wall to make it collapse, ¹⁶ a wise woman called out from the city, "Listen! Listen! Please tell Joab to come here and let me speak with him."

¹⁷ When he had come near her, the woman asked, "Are you Joab?"

"I am," he replied.

"Listen to the words of your servant," she said to him.

He answered, "I'm listening."

¹⁸ She said, "In the past they used to say, 'Seek counsel in Abel,' and that's how they settled disputes. ¹⁹ I am one of the peaceful and faithful in Israel, but you're trying to destroy a city that is like a mother in Israel. Why would you devour the LORD's inheritance?"

²⁰ Joab protested: "Never! I would never devour or demolish! ²¹ That is not the case. There is a man named Sheba son of Bichri, from the hill country of Ephraim, who has rebelled against King David. Deliver this one man, and I will withdraw from the city."

The woman replied to Joab, "Watch! His head will be thrown over the wall to you." ²² The woman went to all the people with her wise counsel, and they cut off the head of Sheba son of Bichri and threw it to Joab. So he blew the ram's horn, and they

dispersed from the city, each to his own tent. Joab returned to the king in Jerusalem.

²³ Joab commanded the whole army of Israel;
Benaiah son of Jehoiada was over the Cherethites and Pelethites;
²⁴ Adoram was over forced labor;
Jehoshaphat son of Ahilud was court historian;
²⁵ Sheva was court secretary;
Zadok and Abiathar were priests;
²⁶ and in addition, Ira the Jairite was David's priest.

Justice for the Gibeonites

21 During David's reign there was a famine for three successive years, so David inquired of the LORD. The LORD answered, "It is due to Saul and to his bloody family, because he killed the Gibeonites."

² The Gibeonites were not Israelites but rather a remnant of the Amorites. The Israelites had taken an oath concerning them, but Saul had tried to kill them in his zeal for the Israelites and Judah. So David summoned the Gibeonites and spoke to them. ³ He asked the Gibeonites, "What should I do for you? How can I make atonement so that you will bring a blessing on the LORD's inheritance?"

⁴ The Gibeonites said to him, "We are not asking for silver and gold from Saul or his family, and we cannot put anyone to death in Israel."

"Whatever you say, I will do for you," he said.

⁵ They replied to the king, "As for the man who annihilated us and plotted to destroy us so we would not exist within the whole territory of Israel, ⁶ let seven of his male descendants be handed over to us so we may hang them in the presence of the LORD at Gibeah of Saul, the LORD's chosen."

The king answered, "I will hand them over."

⁷ David spared Mephibosheth, the son of Saul's son Jonathan, because of the oath of the LORD that was between David and Jonathan, Saul's son. ⁸ But the king took Armoni and Mephibosheth, who were the two sons whom Rizpah daughter of Aiah had borne to Saul, and the five sons whom Merab daughter of Saul had borne to Adriel son of Barzillai the Meholathite ⁹ and handed them over to the Gibeonites. They hanged them on the hill in the presence of the LORD; the seven of them died together. They were executed in the first days of the harvest at the beginning of the barley harvest.

The Burial of Saul's Family

¹⁰ Rizpah, Aiah's daughter, took sackcloth and spread it out for herself on the rock from the beginning of the harvest until the rain poured down from heaven on the bodies. She kept the birds of the sky from them by day and the wild animals by night.

¹¹ When it was reported to David what Saul's concubine Rizpah daughter of Aiah had done, ¹² he went and got the bones of Saul and his son Jonathan from the citizens of Jabesh-gilead. They had stolen them from the public square of Beth-shan where the Philistines had hung the bodies the day the Philistines killed Saul at Gilboa. ¹³ David had the bones brought from there. They gathered up the bones of Saul's family who had been hanged ¹⁴ and buried the bones of Saul and his son Jonathan at Zela in the land of Benjamin in the tomb of Saul's father Kish. They did everything the king commanded. After this, God was receptive to prayer for the land.

The Philistine Giants

¹⁵ The Philistines again waged war against Israel. David went down with his soldiers, and they fought the Philistines, but David became exhausted. ¹⁶ Then Ishbi-benob, one of the

descendants of the giant, whose bronze spear weighed about eight pounds and who wore new armor, intended to kill David. ¹⁷ But Abishai son of Zeruiah came to his aid, struck the Philistine, and killed him. Then David's men swore to him, "You must never again go out with us to battle. You must not extinguish the lamp of Israel."

¹⁸ After this, there was another battle with the Philistines at Gob. At that time Sibbecai the Hushathite killed Saph, who was one of the descendants of the giant.

¹⁹ Once again there was a battle with the Philistines at Gob, and Elhanan son of Jaare-oregim the Bethlehemite killed Goliath of Gath. The shaft of his spear was like a weaver's beam.

²⁰ At Gath there was still another battle. A huge man was there with six fingers on each hand and six toes on each foot — twenty-four in all. He, too, was descended from the giant. ²¹ When he taunted Israel, Jonathan, son of David's brother Shimei, killed him.

²² These four were descended from the giant in Gath and were killed by David and his soldiers.

David's Song of Thanksgiving

22 David spoke the words of this song to the LORD on the day the LORD rescued him from the grasp of all his enemies and from the grasp of Saul. ² He said:

The LORD is my rock, my fortress, and my deliverer,
³ my God, my rock where I seek refuge.
My shield, the horn of my salvation, my stronghold,
    my refuge,
and my Savior, you save me from violence.
⁴ I called to the LORD, who is worthy of praise,
and I was saved from my enemies.
⁵ For the waves of death engulfed me;
the torrents of destruction terrified me.

⁶ The ropes of Sheol entangled me;
the snares of death confronted me.

⁷ I called to the LORD in my distress;
I called to my God.
From his temple he heard my voice,
and my cry for help reached his ears.

⁸ Then the earth shook and quaked;
the foundations of the heavens trembled;
they shook because he burned with anger.

⁹ Smoke rose from his nostrils,
and consuming fire came from his mouth;
coals were set ablaze by it.

¹⁰ He bent the heavens and came down,
total darkness beneath his feet.

¹¹ He rode on a cherub and flew,
soaring on the wings of the wind.

¹² He made darkness a canopy around him,
a gathering of water and thick clouds.

¹³ From the radiance of his presence,
blazing coals were ignited.

¹⁴ The LORD thundered from heaven;
the Most High made his voice heard.

¹⁵ He shot arrows and scattered them;
he hurled lightning bolts and routed them.

¹⁶ The depths of the sea became visible,
the foundations of the world were exposed
at the rebuke of the LORD,
at the blast of the breath of his nostrils.

¹⁷ He reached down from on high
and took hold of me;
he pulled me out of deep water.

18 He rescued me from my powerful enemy
and from those who hated me,
for they were too strong for me.
19 They confronted me in the day of my calamity,
but the LORD was my support.
20 He brought me out to a spacious place;
he rescued me because he delighted in me.

21 The LORD rewarded me
according to my righteousness;
he repaid me
according to the cleanness of my hands.
22 For I have kept the ways of the LORD
and have not turned from my God to wickedness.
23 Indeed, I let all his ordinances guide me
and have not disregarded his statutes.
24 I was blameless before him
and kept myself from my iniquity.
25 So the LORD repaid me
according to my righteousness,
according to my cleanness in his sight.

26 With the faithful
you prove yourself faithful,
with the blameless
you prove yourself blameless,
27 with the pure
you prove yourself pure,
but with the crooked
you prove yourself shrewd.
28 You rescue an oppressed people,
but your eyes are set against the proud —
you humble them.

29 LORD, you are my lamp;
   the LORD illuminates my darkness.
30 With you I can attack a barricade,
   and with my God I can leap over a wall.
31 God — his way is perfect;
   the word of the LORD is pure.
   He is a shield to all who take refuge in him.

32 For who is God besides the LORD?
   And who is a rock? Only our God.
33 God is my strong refuge;
   he makes my way perfect.
34 He makes my feet like the feet of a deer
   and sets me securely on the heights.
35 He trains my hands for war;
   my arms can bend a bow of bronze.
36 You have given me the shield of your salvation;
   your help exalts me.
37 You make a spacious place beneath me for my steps,
   and my ankles do not give way.
38 I pursue my enemies and destroy them;
   I do not turn back until they are wiped out.
39 I wipe them out and crush them,
   and they do not rise;
   they fall beneath my feet.
40 You have clothed me with strength for battle;
   you subdue my adversaries beneath me.
41 You have made my enemies retreat before me;
   I annihilate those who hate me.
42 They look, but there is no one to save them —
   they look to the LORD, but he does not answer them.
43 I pulverize them like dust of the earth;
   I crush them and trample them like mud in the streets.

⁴⁴ You have freed me from the feuds among my people;
    you have preserved me as head of nations;
    a people I had not known serve me.
⁴⁵ Foreigners submit to me cringing;
    as soon as they hear, they obey me.
⁴⁶ Foreigners lose heart
    and come trembling from their fortifications.

⁴⁷ The LORD lives — blessed be my rock!
    God, the rock of my salvation, is exalted.
⁴⁸ God — he grants me vengeance
    and casts down peoples under me.
⁴⁹ He frees me from my enemies.
    You exalt me above my adversaries;
    you rescue me from violent men.

⁵⁰ Therefore I will give thanks to you among
        the nations, LORD;
    I will sing praises about your name.
⁵¹ He is a tower of salvation for his king;
    he shows loyalty to his anointed,
    to David and his descendants forever.

David's Last Words

23 These are the last words of David:
    The declaration of David son of Jesse,
    the declaration of the man raised on high,
    the one anointed by the God of Jacob.
    This is the most delightful of Israel's songs.
² The Spirit of the LORD spoke through me,
    his word was on my tongue.
³ The God of Israel spoke;
    the Rock of Israel said to me,

"The one who rules the people with justice,
who rules in the fear of God,
⁴ is like the morning light when the sun rises
on a cloudless morning,
the glisten of rain on sprouting grass."

⁵ Is it not true my house is with God?
For he has established a permanent covenant with me,
ordered and secured in every detail.
Will he not bring about
my whole salvation and my every desire?
⁶ But all the wicked are like thorns raked aside;
they can never be picked up by hand.
⁷ The man who touches them
must be armed with iron and the shaft of a spear.
They will be completely burned up on the spot.

Exploits of David's Warriors

⁸ These are the names of David's warriors:

Josheb-basshebeth the Tahchemonite was chief of the officers. He wielded his spear against eight hundred men that he killed at one time.

⁹ After him, Eleazar son of Dodo son of an Ahohite was among the three warriors with David when they defied the Philistines. The men of Israel retreated in the place they had gathered for battle, ¹⁰ but Eleazar stood his ground and attacked the Philistines until his hand was tired and stuck to his sword. The LORD brought about a great victory that day. Then the troops came back to him, but only to plunder the dead.

¹¹ After him was Shammah son of Agee the Hararite. The Philistines had assembled in formation where there was a field full of lentils. The troops fled from the Philistines, ¹² but Shammah took his stand in the middle of the field, defended it, and

struck down the Philistines. So the LORD brought about a great victory.

¹³ Three of the thirty leading warriors went down at harvest time and came to David at the cave of Adullam, while a company of Philistines was camping in Rephaim Valley. ¹⁴ At that time David was in the stronghold, and a Philistine garrison was at Bethlehem. ¹⁵ David was extremely thirsty and said, "If only someone would bring me water to drink from the well at the city gate of Bethlehem!" ¹⁶ So three of the warriors broke through the Philistine camp and drew water from the well at the gate of Bethlehem. They brought it back to David, but he refused to drink it. Instead, he poured it out to the LORD. ¹⁷ David said, "LORD, I would never do such a thing! Is this not the blood of men who risked their lives?" So he refused to drink it. Such were the exploits of the three warriors.

¹⁸ Abishai, Joab's brother and son of Zeruiah, was leader of the Three. He wielded his spear against three hundred men and killed them, gaining a reputation among the Three. ¹⁹ Was he not more honored than the Three? He became their commander even though he did not become one of the Three.

²⁰ Benaiah son of Jehoiada was the son of a brave man from Kabzeel, a man of many exploits. Benaiah killed two sons of Ariel of Moab, and he went down into a pit on a snowy day and killed a lion. ²¹ He also killed an Egyptian, an impressive man. Even though the Egyptian had a spear in his hand, Benaiah went down to him with a staff, snatched the spear out of the Egyptian's hand, and then killed him with his own spear. ²² These were the exploits of Benaiah son of Jehoiada, who had a reputation among the three warriors. ²³ He was the most honored of the Thirty, but he did not become one of the Three. David put him in charge of his bodyguard.

²⁴ Among the Thirty were
    Joab's brother Asahel,

Elhanan son of Dodo of Bethlehem,
25 Shammah the Harodite,
Elika the Harodite,
26 Helez the Paltite,
Ira son of Ikkesh the Tekoite,
27 Abiezer the Anathothite,
Mebunnai the Hushathite,
28 Zalmon the Ahohite,
Maharai the Netophathite,
29 Heleb son of Baanah the Netophathite,
Ittai son of Ribai from Gibeah
of the Benjaminites,
30 Benaiah the Pirathonite,
Hiddai from the wadis of Gaash,
31 Abi-albon the Arbathite,
Azmaveth the Barhumite,
32 Eliahba the Shaalbonite,
the sons of Jashen,
Jonathan son of 33 Shammah the Hararite,
Ahiam son of Sharar the Hararite,
34 Eliphelet son of Ahasbai son of the Maacathite,
Eliam son of Ahithophel the Gilonite,
35 Hezro the Carmelite,
Paarai the Arbite,
36 Igal son of Nathan from Zobah,
Bani the Gadite,
37 Zelek the Ammonite,
Naharai the Beerothite, the armor-bearer for Joab
son of Zeruiah,
38 Ira the Ithrite,
Gareb the Ithrite,
39 and Uriah the Hethite.
There were thirty-seven in all.

David's Military Census

24 The LORD's anger burned against Israel again, and he stirred up David against them to say, "Go, count the people of Israel and Judah."

² So the king said to Joab, the commander of his army, "Go through all the tribes of Israel from Dan to Beer-sheba and register the troops so I can know their number."

³ Joab replied to the king, "May the LORD your God multiply the troops a hundred times more than they are — while my lord the king looks on! But why does my lord the king want to do this?"

⁴ Yet the king's order prevailed over Joab and the commanders of the army. So Joab and the commanders of the army left the king's presence to register the troops of Israel.

⁵ They crossed the Jordan and camped in Aroer, south of the town in the middle of the valley, and then proceeded toward Gad and Jazer. ⁶ They went to Gilead and to the land of the Hittites and continued on to Dan-jaan and around to Sidon. ⁷ They went to the fortress of Tyre and all the cities of the Hivites and Canaanites. Afterward, they went to the Negev of Judah at Beer-sheba.

⁸ When they had gone through the whole land, they returned to Jerusalem at the end of nine months and twenty days. ⁹ Joab gave the king the total of the registration of the troops. There were eight hundred thousand valiant armed men from Israel and five hundred thousand men from Judah.

¹⁰ David's conscience troubled him after he had taken a census of the troops. He said to the LORD, "I have sinned greatly in what I've done. Now, LORD, because I've been very foolish, please take away your servant's guilt."

David's Punishment

¹¹ When David got up in the morning, the word of the LORD had come to the prophet Gad, David's seer: ¹² "Go and say to David,

'This is what the Lord says: I am offering you three choices. Choose one of them, and I will do it to you.'"

¹³ So Gad went to David, told him the choices, and asked him, "Do you want three years of famine to come on your land, to flee from your foes three months while they pursue you, or to have a plague in your land three days? Now, consider carefully what answer I should take back to the one who sent me."

¹⁴ David answered Gad, "I have great anxiety. Please, let us fall into the Lord's hands because his mercies are great, but don't let me fall into human hands."

¹⁵ So the Lord sent a plague on Israel from that morning until the appointed time, and from Dan to Beer-sheba seventy thousand men died. ¹⁶ Then the angel extended his hand toward Jerusalem to destroy it, but the Lord relented concerning the destruction and said to the angel who was destroying the people, "Enough, withdraw your hand now!" The angel of the Lord was then at the threshing floor of Araunah the Jebusite.

¹⁷ When David saw the angel striking the people, he said to the Lord, "Look, I am the one who has sinned; I am the one who has done wrong. But these sheep, what have they done? Please, let your hand be against me and my father's family."

David's Altar

¹⁸ Gad came to David that day and said to him, "Go up and set up an altar to the Lord on the threshing floor of Araunah the Jebusite." ¹⁹ David went up in obedience to Gad's command, just as the Lord had commanded. ²⁰ Araunah looked down and saw the king and his servants coming toward him, so he went out and paid homage to the king with his face to the ground.

²¹ Araunah said, "Why has my lord the king come to his servant?"

David replied, "To buy the threshing floor from you in order to build an altar to the LORD, so the plague on the people may be halted."

²² Araunah said to David, "My lord the king may take whatever he wants and offer it. Here are the oxen for a burnt offering and the threshing sledges and ox yokes for the wood. ²³ Your Majesty, Araunah gives everything here to the king." Then he said to the king, "May the LORD your God accept you."

²⁴ The king answered Araunah, "No, I insist on buying it from you for a price, for I will not offer to the LORD my God burnt offerings that cost me nothing." David bought the threshing floor and the oxen for twenty ounces of silver. ²⁵ He built an altar to the LORD there and offered burnt offerings and fellowship offerings. Then the LORD was receptive to prayer for the land, and the plague on Israel ended.